TEACHER'S PET PUBLICATIONS

PUZZLE PACK
for
Adventures of Huckleberry Finn
based on the book by
Mark Twain

Written by
William T. Collins

© 2005 Teacher's Pet Publications
All Rights Reserved

The materials in this packet are copyrighted
by Teacher's Pet Publications, Inc.

These pages may be duplicated by the purchaser
for use in the purchaser's own classroom.

Copying any of these materials and distributing them
for any other purpose is a violation of the copyright laws.

© 2005 Teacher's Pet Publications, Inc.
www.tpet.com

INTRODUCTION
If you already own the LitPlan for this title, this Puzzle Pack will refresh your Unit Resource Materials and Vocabulary Resource Materials sections plus give you additional materials you can substitute into the tests. If you do not already have a complete LitPlan, these pages will give you some supplemental materials to use with your own plan. There are two main groups of materials: one set for unit words (such as characters' names, symbols, places, etc.) and one set for vocabulary words associated with the book.

WORD LIST
There is a word list for both the unit words and the vocabulary words. These lists show you which words are being used in the materials and the clues or definitions being used for those words. You may want to give students a word list with clues/definitions to help them, or you may want students to only have a word list (without clues/definitions) if you want them to work a little harder. Both are available for duplication. The word lists can also be your "calling key" for the bingo games.

FILL IN THE BLANK AND MATCHING
There are 4 each of the fill in the blank and matching worksheets for both the unit and vocabulary words. These pages can be used either as extra worksheets for students or as objective parts of a unit test. They can be done individually if students need extra help or as a whole class activity to review the material covered.

MAGIC SQUARES
The magic squares not only reinforce the material covered but also work on reasoning and math skills. Many teachers have told us that their students really enjoy doing these!

WORD SEARCH PUZZLES
The word search words go in all directions, as indicated on your answer keys. Two of the word search puzzles have the clues listed rather than the words. This makes the puzzle a little more difficult, but it reinforces the material better. Two word search puzzles have words only for students who find the clue puzzles too difficult.

CROSSWORD PUZZLES
Both unit and vocabulary word sections have 4 crossword puzzles.

BINGO CARDS
There are 32 individual bingo cards for the unit words and 32 individual bingo cards for the vocabulary words. You can use your word list as a "call list," calling the words at random and marking them off of your list as you go, or you could use the flash cards by cutting them apart and drawing the words at random from a hat (or box or whatever). To make a better review, you might ask for the definition and spelling of each word as you call it out–or you could call out the definitions and have students tell you the words they need to look for on the puzzle.

JUGGLE LETTERS
The vocabulary juggle letter game is intended to help students learn the spellings of the words. One sheet has the definitions listed on it as an extra help for students who need it or to reinforce the definitions if you choose to do so.

FLASH CARDS
We've included a set of vocabulary flash cards you can duplicate, cut, and fold for your students. Some teachers make a few sets for general use by the class; others make a set for each student. Some teachers duplicate them for each student and have the students cut & fold their own. You can cut out just the words and put them in a hat, have each student pick out one word and write the definition and a sentence for that word. Students then swap words and papers, with the next student adding a sentence of his own under the last one. You can have students swap as many times as you like. Each time the student will read the sentences written prior to his own and then add a sentence. You can cut out the words and definitions separately and play "I Have; Who Has?" Each student in the room draws a word and definition. The first student says, "I have (the name of the word). Who has the definition?" The student with the definition reads it then says, "I have (the name of the vocabulary word she has). Who has the definition?" The round continues until all words and definitions have been given.

Huck Finn Word List

No.	Word	Clue/Definition
1.	BOGGS	Col. Sherburn shot him.
2.	BUCK	Grangerford boy Huck's age
3.	CABIN	Huck and Jim found a dead man in one.
4.	CIVILIZED	Conforming to rules of society
5.	CLEMENS	A.K.A. Twain
6.	COFFIN	Huck hides money there.
7.	EDUCATION	Widow Douglas thinks Huck should get this at school.
8.	ESCAPE	Tom and Huck help Jim do this.
9.	FISHING	Huck's hook and line pastime
10.	FREEDOM	Opposite of slavery
11.	GANG	Tom Sawyer was the leader of a ___ of boys.
12.	GRANGERFORDS	They feud with the Shepherdsons.
13.	HAIRBALL	The ___ Oracle
14.	HANNIBAL	Twain's hometown
15.	HARKNESS	Leads the mob against Col. Sherburn
16.	HARNEY	Buck shot at this Shepherdson.
17.	HOG	Huck uses the blood of one to stage his own death.
18.	HUCK	Narrator
19.	ISLAND	Jackson's ___
20.	JIM	He told Huck many superstitions.
21.	KING	Solomon, for example
22.	LOFTUS	Huck visits her in town, dressed as a girl.
23.	LUCK	It can be bad or good: fate
24.	MATTRESS	King & Duke hide money there.
25.	MISSISSIPPI	River on which Huck and Jim traveled
26.	MISSOURI	Hannibal's state
27.	MOSES	I Discover ___ And The Bulrushers
28.	NATURE	Theme relating to outdoors
29.	OATH	Pledge
30.	PAP	Mr. Finn to Huck
31.	POLLY	Tom's aunt and guardian
32.	RAFT	Huck's river transportation
33.	RELIGION	Widow Douglas thinks Huck should get this at church.
34.	RIVERBOATS	They transported goods and people on the Mississippi.
35.	SALLY	Mrs. Phelps; Tom's aunt
36.	SARAH	Huck's girl name
37.	SILAS	Mr. Phelps
38.	SLAVE	Jim's relationship to Miss Watson
39.	SNAKE	One bit Jim.
40.	THATCHER	The judge
41.	TOM	Huck's dreamer friend
42.	TURNER	Packard & Bill plot to kill him.
43.	TWAIN	Author Mark ___
44.	WALTER	___ Scott
45.	WATSON	Sister to Widow Douglas
46.	WHISKEY	Pap's drink
47.	WIDOW	Marital status of the Douglas woman
48.	WILKS	Dead Peter's last name

Huck Finn Fill In The Blanks 1

_____ 1. Pap's drink

_____ 2. A.K.A. Twain

_____ 3. Solomon, for example

_____ 4. Tom's aunt and guardian

_____ 5. King & Duke hide money there.

_____ 6. Theme relating to outdoors

_____ 7. Mr. Finn to Huck

_____ 8. The ___ Oracle

_____ 9. Huck uses the blood of one to stage his own death.

_____ 10. I Discover ___ And The Bulrushers

_____ 11. It can be bad or good: fate

_____ 12. Conforming to rules of society

_____ 13. Leads the mob against Col. Sherburn

_____ 14. Mrs. Phelps; Tom's aunt

_____ 15. They feud with the Shepherdsons.

_____ 16. Huck visits her in town, dressed as a girl.

_____ 17. Tom and Huck help Jim do this.

_____ 18. Jim's relationship to Miss Watson

_____ 19. Huck hides money there.

_____ 20. Widow Douglas thinks Huck should get this at church.

Huck Finn Fill In The Blanks 1 Answer Key

Answer	Clue
WHISKEY	1. Pap's drink
CLEMENS	2. A.K.A. Twain
KING	3. Solomon, for example
POLLY	4. Tom's aunt and guardian
MATTRESS	5. King & Duke hide money there.
NATURE	6. Theme relating to outdoors
PAP	7. Mr. Finn to Huck
HAIRBALL	8. The ___ Oracle
HOG	9. Huck uses the blood of one to stage his own death.
MOSES	10. I Discover ___ And The Bulrushers
LUCK	11. It can be bad or good: fate
CIVILIZED	12. Conforming to rules of society
HARKNESS	13. Leads the mob against Col. Sherburn
SALLY	14. Mrs. Phelps; Tom's aunt
GRANGERFORDS	15. They feud with the Shepherdsons.
LOFTUS	16. Huck visits her in town, dressed as a girl.
ESCAPE	17. Tom and Huck help Jim do this.
SLAVE	18. Jim's relationship to Miss Watson
COFFIN	19. Huck hides money there.
RELIGION	20. Widow Douglas thinks Huck should get this at church.

Huck Finn Fill In The Blanks 2

_____

1. Solomon, for example
2. The judge
3. River on which Huck and Jim traveled
4. Huck's river transportation
5. Marital status of the Douglas woman
6. Author Mark ___
7. Huck's hook and line pastime
8. They feud with the Shepherdsons.
9. It can be bad or good: fate
10. Theme relating to outdoors
11. They transported goods and people on the Mississippi.
12. Hannibal's state
13. Huck's girl name
14. I Discover ___ And The Bulrushers
15. Widow Douglas thinks Huck should get this at church.
16. Tom and Huck help Jim do this.
17. Huck's dreamer friend
18. Huck and Jim found a dead man in one.
19. Opposite of slavery
20. Tom's aunt and guardian

Huck Finn Fill In The Blanks 2 Answer Key

KING	1. Solomon, for example
THATCHER	2. The judge
MISSISSIPPI	3. River on which Huck and Jim traveled
RAFT	4. Huck's river transportation
WIDOW	5. Marital status of the Douglas woman
TWAIN	6. Author Mark ___
FISHING	7. Huck's hook and line pastime
GRANGERFORDS	8. They feud with the Shepherdsons.
LUCK	9. It can be bad or good: fate
NATURE	10. Theme relating to outdoors
RIVERBOATS	11. They transported goods and people on the Mississippi.
MISSOURI	12. Hannibal's state
SARAH	13. Huck's girl name
MOSES	14. I Discover ___ And The Bulrushers
RELIGION	15. Widow Douglas thinks Huck should get this at church.
ESCAPE	16. Tom and Huck help Jim do this.
TOM	17. Huck's dreamer friend
CABIN	18. Huck and Jim found a dead man in one.
FREEDOM	19. Opposite of slavery
POLLY	20. Tom's aunt and guardian

Huck Finn Fill In The Blanks 3

1. Packard & Bill plot to kill him.
2. Widow Douglas thinks Huck should get this at church.
3. King & Duke hide money there.
4. Author Mark ___
5. Tom Sawyer was the leader of a ___ of boys.
6. Huck's river transportation
7. Opposite of slavery
8. He told Huck many superstitions.
9. Pledge
10. Solomon, for example
11. It can be bad or good: fate
12. Tom and Huck help Jim do this.
13. Mr. Phelps
14. Marital status of the Douglas woman
15. Pap's drink
16. River on which Huck and Jim traveled
17. Mr. Finn to Huck
18. Twain's hometown
19. They feud with the Shepherdsons.
20. Huck's dreamer friend

Huck Finn Fill In The Blanks 3 Answer Key

TURNER	1. Packard & Bill plot to kill him.
RELIGION	2. Widow Douglas thinks Huck should get this at church.
MATTRESS	3. King & Duke hide money there.
TWAIN	4. Author Mark ___
GANG	5. Tom Sawyer was the leader of a ___ of boys.
RAFT	6. Huck's river transportation
FREEDOM	7. Opposite of slavery
JIM	8. He told Huck many superstitions.
OATH	9. Pledge
KING	10. Solomon, for example
LUCK	11. It can be bad or good: fate
ESCAPE	12. Tom and Huck help Jim do this.
SILAS	13. Mr. Phelps
WIDOW	14. Marital status of the Douglas woman
WHISKEY	15. Pap's drink
MISSISSIPPI	16. River on which Huck and Jim traveled
PAP	17. Mr. Finn to Huck
HANNIBAL	18. Twain's hometown
GRANGERFORDS	19. They feud with the Shepherdsons.
TOM	20. Huck's dreamer friend

Huck Finn Fill In The Blanks 4

_____

1. Conforming to rules of society
2. Tom's aunt and guardian
3. River on which Huck and Jim traveled
4. Author Mark ___
5. They transported goods and people on the Mississippi.
6. Pledge
7. Col. Sherburn shot him.
8. Grangerford boy Huck's age
9. King & Duke hide money there.
10. Jim's relationship to Miss Watson
11. Tom Sawyer was the leader of a ___ of boys.
12. Twain's hometown
13. The judge
14. Packard & Bill plot to kill him.
15. Huck's river transportation
16. ___ Scott
17. Huck's hook and line pastime
18. Mr. Finn to Huck
19. Huck uses the blood of one to stage his own death.
20. Huck visits her in town, dressed as a girl.

Huck Finn Fill In The Blanks 4 Answer Key

CIVILIZED	1. Conforming to rules of society
POLLY	2. Tom's aunt and guardian
MISSISSIPPI	3. River on which Huck and Jim traveled
TWAIN	4. Author Mark ___
RIVERBOATS	5. They transported goods and people on the Mississippi.
OATH	6. Pledge
BOGGS	7. Col. Sherburn shot him.
BUCK	8. Grangerford boy Huck's age
MATTRESS	9. King & Duke hide money there.
SLAVE	10. Jim's relationship to Miss Watson
GANG	11. Tom Sawyer was the leader of a ___ of boys.
HANNIBAL	12. Twain's hometown
THATCHER	13. The judge
TURNER	14. Packard & Bill plot to kill him.
RAFT	15. Huck's river transportation
WALTER	16. ___ Scott
FISHING	17. Huck's hook and line pastime
PAP	18. Mr. Finn to Huck
HOG	19. Huck uses the blood of one to stage his own death.
LOFTUS	20. Huck visits her in town, dressed as a girl.

Huck Finn Matching 1

___ 1. GANG   A. Twain's hometown
___ 2. KING   B. I Discover ___ And The Bulrushers
___ 3. ISLAND   C. Buck shot at this Shepherdson.
___ 4. GRANGERFORDS D. The ___ Oracle
___ 5. SARAH   E. Jackson's ___
___ 6. CIVILIZED   F. Widow Douglas thinks Huck should get this at school.
___ 7. SLAVE   G. Huck and Jim found a dead man in one.
___ 8. SILAS   H. Huck uses the blood of one to stage his own death.
___ 9. EDUCATION   I. They transported goods and people on the Mississippi.
___10. MATTRESS   J. They feud with the Shepherdsons.
___11. HANNIBAL   K. Tom Sawyer was the leader of a ___ of boys.
___12. MOSES   L. The judge
___13. HOG   M. Mrs. Phelps; Tom's aunt
___14. THATCHER   N. Huck's hook and line pastime
___15. CABIN   O. Huck's dreamer friend
___16. SALLY   P. Conforming to rules of society
___17. TOM   Q. Jim's relationship to Miss Watson
___18. LUCK   R. King & Duke hide money there.
___19. CLEMENS   S. It can be bad or good: fate
___20. FISHING   T. A.K.A. Twain
___21. BOGGS   U. Solomon, for example
___22. RIVERBOATS   V. Huck's girl name
___23. HARKNESS   W. Mr. Phelps
___24. HARNEY   X. Leads the mob against Col. Sherburn
___25. HAIRBALL   Y. Col. Sherburn shot him.

Huck Finn Matching 1 Answer Key

K - 1. GANG	A. Twain's hometown
U - 2. KING	B. I Discover ___ And The Bulrushers
E - 3. ISLAND	C. Buck shot at this Shepherdson.
J - 4. GRANGERFORDS	D. The ___ Oracle
V - 5. SARAH	E. Jackson's ___
P - 6. CIVILIZED	F. Widow Douglas thinks Huck should get this at school.
Q - 7. SLAVE	G. Huck and Jim found a dead man in one.
W - 8. SILAS	H. Huck uses the blood of one to stage his own death.
F - 9. EDUCATION	I. They transported goods and people on the Mississippi.
R -10. MATTRESS	J. They feud with the Shepherdsons.
A -11. HANNIBAL	K. Tom Sawyer was the leader of a ___ of boys.
B -12. MOSES	L. The judge
H -13. HOG	M. Mrs. Phelps; Tom's aunt
L -14. THATCHER	N. Huck's hook and line pastime
G -15. CABIN	O. Huck's dreamer friend
M -16. SALLY	P. Conforming to rules of society
O -17. TOM	Q. Jim's relationship to Miss Watson
S -18. LUCK	R. King & Duke hide money there.
T -19. CLEMENS	S. It can be bad or good: fate
N -20. FISHING	T. A.K.A. Twain
Y -21. BOGGS	U. Solomon, for example
I - 22. RIVERBOATS	V. Huck's girl name
X -23. HARKNESS	W. Mr. Phelps
C -24. HARNEY	X. Leads the mob against Col. Sherburn
D -25. HAIRBALL	Y. Col. Sherburn shot him.

Huck Finn Matching 2

___ 1. FREEDOM
___ 2. ISLAND
___ 3. TURNER
___ 4. SLAVE
___ 5. COFFIN
___ 6. NATURE
___ 7. WIDOW
___ 8. GRANGERFORDS
___ 9. ESCAPE
___ 10. WHISKEY
___ 11. CABIN
___ 12. EDUCATION
___ 13. WATSON
___ 14. HANNIBAL
___ 15. HOG
___ 16. BOGGS
___ 17. MOSES
___ 18. WILKS
___ 19. MATTRESS
___ 20. RELIGION
___ 21. HARNEY
___ 22. HUCK
___ 23. SILAS
___ 24. HARKNESS
___ 25. KING

A. Leads the mob against Col. Sherburn
B. Col. Sherburn shot him.
C. Narrator
D. Tom and Huck help Jim do this.
E. Dead Peter's last name
F. Packard & Bill plot to kill him.
G. King & Duke hide money there.
H. Huck and Jim found a dead man in one.
I. Jackson's ___
J. Jim's relationship to Miss Watson
K. Pap's drink
L. Marital status of the Douglas woman
M. I Discover ___ And The Bulrushers
N. Solomon, for example
O. Huck hides money there.
P. Huck uses the blood of one to stage his own death.
Q. Opposite of slavery
R. Theme relating to outdoors
S. Widow Douglas thinks Huck should get this at church.
T. Twain's hometown
U. Sister to Widow Douglas
V. Widow Douglas thinks Huck should get this at school.
W. Mr. Phelps
X. Buck shot at this Shepherdson.
Y. They feud with the Shepherdsons.

Huck Finn Matching 2 Answer Key

Q - 1. FREEDOM   A. Leads the mob against Col. Sherburn
I - 2. ISLAND   B. Col. Sherburn shot him.
F - 3. TURNER   C. Narrator
J - 4. SLAVE   D. Tom and Huck help Jim do this.
O - 5. COFFIN   E. Dead Peter's last name
R - 6. NATURE   F. Packard & Bill plot to kill him.
L - 7. WIDOW   G. King & Duke hide money there.
Y - 8. GRANGERFORDS   H. Huck and Jim found a dead man in one.
D - 9. ESCAPE   I. Jackson's ___
K - 10. WHISKEY   J. Jim's relationship to Miss Watson
H - 11. CABIN   K. Pap's drink
V - 12. EDUCATION   L. Marital status of the Douglas woman
U - 13. WATSON   M. I Discover ___ And The Bulrushers
T - 14. HANNIBAL   N. Solomon, for example
P - 15. HOG   O. Huck hides money there.
B - 16. BOGGS   P. Huck uses the blood of one to stage his own death.
M - 17. MOSES   Q. Opposite of slavery
E - 18. WILKS   R. Theme relating to outdoors
G - 19. MATTRESS   S. Widow Douglas thinks Huck should get this at church.
S - 20. RELIGION   T. Twain's hometown
X - 21. HARNEY   U. Sister to Widow Douglas
C - 22. HUCK   V. Widow Douglas thinks Huck should get this at school.
W - 23. SILAS   W. Mr. Phelps
A - 24. HARKNESS   X. Buck shot at this Shepherdson.
N - 25. KING   Y. They feud with the Shepherdsons.

Huck Finn Matching 3

___ 1. SARAH   A. Tom and Huck help Jim do this.
___ 2. HANNIBAL   B. Huck hides money there.
___ 3. COFFIN   C. King & Duke hide money there.
___ 4. GRANGERFORDS   D. Jackson's ___
___ 5. WIDOW   E. Opposite of slavery
___ 6. HUCK   F. Solomon, for example
___ 7. BUCK   G. Grangerford boy Huck's age
___ 8. SALLY   H. Huck's girl name
___ 9. ISLAND   I. Hannibal's state
___10. TOM   J. Pap's drink
___11. CABIN   K. One bit Jim.
___12. SNAKE   L. A.K.A. Twain
___13. BOGGS   M. Marital status of the Douglas woman
___14. RELIGION   N. Twain's hometown
___15. KING   O. The ___ Oracle
___16. HAIRBALL   P. Col. Sherburn shot him.
___17. MISSOURI   Q. The judge
___18. THATCHER   R. They feud with the Shepherdsons.
___19. WHISKEY   S. Narrator
___20. CLEMENS   T. Huck's hook and line pastime
___21. MATTRESS   U. Huck's dreamer friend
___22. WILKS   V. Mrs. Phelps; Tom's aunt
___23. ESCAPE   W. Dead Peter's last name
___24. FISHING   X. Widow Douglas thinks Huck should get this at church.
___25. FREEDOM   Y. Huck and Jim found a dead man in one.

Huck Finn Matching 3 Answer Key

H - 1. SARAH	A. Tom and Huck help Jim do this.
N - 2. HANNIBAL	B. Huck hides money there.
B - 3. COFFIN	C. King & Duke hide money there.
R - 4. GRANGERFORDS	D. Jackson's ___
M - 5. WIDOW	E. Opposite of slavery
S - 6. HUCK	F. Solomon, for example
G - 7. BUCK	G. Grangerford boy Huck's age
V - 8. SALLY	H. Huck's girl name
D - 9. ISLAND	I. Hannibal's state
U - 10. TOM	J. Pap's drink
Y - 11. CABIN	K. One bit Jim.
K - 12. SNAKE	L. A.K.A. Twain
P - 13. BOGGS	M. Marital status of the Douglas woman
X - 14. RELIGION	N. Twain's hometown
F - 15. KING	O. The ___ Oracle
O - 16. HAIRBALL	P. Col. Sherburn shot him.
I - 17. MISSOURI	Q. The judge
Q - 18. THATCHER	R. They feud with the Shepherdsons.
J - 19. WHISKEY	S. Narrator
L - 20. CLEMENS	T. Huck's hook and line pastime
C - 21. MATTRESS	U. Huck's dreamer friend
W - 22. WILKS	V. Mrs. Phelps; Tom's aunt
A - 23. ESCAPE	W. Dead Peter's last name
T - 24. FISHING	X. Widow Douglas thinks Huck should get this at church.
E - 25. FREEDOM	Y. Huck and Jim found a dead man in one.

Huck Finn Matching 4

___ 1. ESCAPE A. The ___ Oracle
___ 2. SNAKE B. King & Duke hide money there.
___ 3. FREEDOM C. Jim's relationship to Miss Watson
___ 4. HOG D. Tom Sawyer was the leader of a ___ of boys.
___ 5. LOFTUS E. Packard & Bill plot to kill him.
___ 6. SLAVE F. Huck visits her in town, dressed as a girl.
___ 7. COFFIN G. ___ Scott
___ 8. RIVERBOATS H. Huck uses the blood of one to stage his own death.
___ 9. CLEMENS I. Narrator
___ 10. WALTER J. Conforming to rules of society
___ 11. HANNIBAL K. Tom and Huck help Jim do this.
___ 12. MATTRESS L. Col. Sherburn shot him.
___ 13. MISSISSIPPI M. Huck's dreamer friend
___ 14. GANG N. They transported goods and people on the Mississippi.
___ 15. CIVILIZED O. One bit Jim.
___ 16. HARKNESS P. Huck hides money there.
___ 17. TOM Q. Jackson's ___
___ 18. MOSES R. Mr. Finn to Huck
___ 19. ISLAND S. Twain's hometown
___ 20. HAIRBALL T. Leads the mob against Col. Sherburn
___ 21. TURNER U. Opposite of slavery
___ 22. THATCHER V. River on which Huck and Jim traveled
___ 23. BOGGS W. I Discover ___ And The Bulrushers
___ 24. HUCK X. The judge
___ 25. PAP Y. A.K.A. Twain

Huck Finn Matching 4 Answer Key

K - 1. ESCAPE	A. The ___ Oracle
O - 2. SNAKE	B. King & Duke hide money there.
U - 3. FREEDOM	C. Jim's relationship to Miss Watson
H - 4. HOG	D. Tom Sawyer was the leader of a ___ of boys.
F - 5. LOFTUS	E. Packard & Bill plot to kill him.
C - 6. SLAVE	F. Huck visits her in town, dressed as a girl.
P - 7. COFFIN	G. ___ Scott
N - 8. RIVERBOATS	H. Huck uses the blood of one to stage his own death.
Y - 9. CLEMENS	I. Narrator
G - 10. WALTER	J. Conforming to rules of society
S - 11. HANNIBAL	K. Tom and Huck help Jim do this.
B - 12. MATTRESS	L. Col. Sherburn shot him.
V - 13. MISSISSIPPI	M. Huck's dreamer friend
D - 14. GANG	N. They transported goods and people on the Mississippi.
J - 15. CIVILIZED	O. One bit Jim.
T - 16. HARKNESS	P. Huck hides money there.
M - 17. TOM	Q. Jackson's ___
W - 18. MOSES	R. Mr. Finn to Huck
Q - 19. ISLAND	S. Twain's hometown
A - 20. HAIRBALL	T. Leads the mob against Col. Sherburn
E - 21. TURNER	U. Opposite of slavery
X - 22. THATCHER	V. River on which Huck and Jim traveled
L - 23. BOGGS	W. I Discover ___ And The Bulrushers
I - 24. HUCK	X. The judge
R - 25. PAP	Y. A.K.A. Twain

Huck Finn Magic Squares 1

Match the definition with the vocabulary word. Put your answers in the magic squares below. When your answers are correct, all columns and rows will add to the same number.

A. TOM
B. HOG
C. WALTER
D. RAFT
E. TWAIN
F. RELIGION
G. THATCHER
H. CLEMENS
I. MISSOURI
J. HANNIBAL
K. SALLY
L. ISLAND
M. WIDOW
N. FREEDOM
O. TURNER
P. MATTRESS

1. Widow Douglas thinks Huck should get this at church.
2. Hannibal's state
3. Packard & Bill plot to kill him.
4. Huck's river transportation
5. Marital status of the Douglas woman
6. Huck uses the blood of one to stage his own death.
7. A.K.A. Twain
8. Mrs. Phelps; Tom's aunt
9. ___ Scott
10. King & Duke hide money there.
11. Twain's hometown
12. Author Mark ___
13. Jackson's ___
14. The judge
15. Huck's dreamer friend
16. Opposite of slavery

A=	B=	C=	D=
E=	F=	G=	H=
I=	J=	K=	L=
M=	N=	O=	P=

Huck Finn Magic Squares 1 Answer Key

Match the definition with the vocabulary word. Put your answers in the magic squares below. When your answers are correct, all columns and rows will add to the same number.

A. TOM
B. HOG
C. WALTER
D. RAFT
E. TWAIN
F. RELIGION
G. THATCHER
H. CLEMENS
I. MISSOURI
J. HANNIBAL
K. SALLY
L. ISLAND
M. WIDOW
N. FREEDOM
O. TURNER
P. MATTRESS

1. Widow Douglas thinks Huck should get this at church.
2. Hannibal's state
3. Packard & Bill plot to kill him.
4. Huck's river transportation
5. Marital status of the Douglas woman
6. Huck uses the blood of one to stage his own death.
7. A.K.A. Twain
8. Mrs. Phelps; Tom's aunt
9. ___ Scott
10. King & Duke hide money there.
11. Twain's hometown
12. Author Mark ___
13. Jackson's ___
14. The judge
15. Huck's dreamer friend
16. Opposite of slavery

A=15	B=6	C=9	D=4
E=12	F=1	G=14	H=7
I=2	J=11	K=8	L=13
M=5	N=16	O=3	P=10

Huck Finn Magic Squares 2

Match the definition with the vocabulary word. Put your answers in the magic squares below. When your answers are correct, all columns and rows will add to the same number.

A. MISSOURI
B. RELIGION
C. POLLY
D. NATURE
E. WHISKEY
F. COFFIN
G. LUCK
H. THATCHER
I. FREEDOM
J. HARNEY
K. KING
L. CABIN
M. WIDOW
N. SNAKE
O. HUCK
P. FISHING

1. The judge
2. Hannibal's state
3. Widow Douglas thinks Huck should get this at church.
4. It can be bad or good: fate
5. Buck shot at this Shepherdson.
6. Narrator
7. Huck's hook and line pastime
8. Opposite of slavery
9. Solomon, for example
10. One bit Jim.
11. Marital status of the Douglas woman
12. Huck and Jim found a dead man in one.
13. Pap's drink
14. Theme relating to outdoors
15. Tom's aunt and guardian
16. Huck hides money there.

A=	B=	C=	D=
E=	F=	G=	H=
I=	J=	K=	L=
M=	N=	O=	P=

Huck Finn Magic Squares 2 Answer Key

Match the definition with the vocabulary word. Put your answers in the magic squares below. When your answers are correct, all columns and rows will add to the same number.

A. MISSOURI
B. RELIGION
C. POLLY
D. NATURE
E. WHISKEY
F. COFFIN
G. LUCK
H. THATCHER
I. FREEDOM
J. HARNEY
K. KING
L. CABIN
M. WIDOW
N. SNAKE
O. HUCK
P. FISHING

1. The judge
2. Hannibal's state
3. Widow Douglas thinks Huck should get this at church.
4. It can be bad or good: fate
5. Buck shot at this Shepherdson.
6. Narrator
7. Huck's hook and line pastime
8. Opposite of slavery
9. Solomon, for example
10. One bit Jim.
11. Marital status of the Douglas woman
12. Huck and Jim found a dead man in one.
13. Pap's drink
14. Theme relating to outdoors
15. Tom's aunt and guardian
16. Huck hides money there.

A=2	B=3	C=15	D=14
E=13	F=16	G=4	H=1
I=8	J=5	K=9	L=12
M=11	N=10	O=6	P=7

Huck Finn Magic Squares 3

Match the definition with the vocabulary word. Put your answers in the magic squares below. When your answers are correct, all columns and rows will add to the same number.

A. CIVILIZED
B. WALTER
C. MATTRESS
D. SLAVE
E. HARKNESS
F. BOGGS
G. KING
H. TURNER
I. EDUCATION
J. BUCK
K. HUCK
L. RELIGION
M. CLEMENS
N. NATURE
O. TWAIN
P. OATH

1. A.K.A. Twain
2. Col. Sherburn shot him.
3. Packard & Bill plot to kill him.
4. Author Mark ___
5. Widow Douglas thinks Huck should get this at church.
6. King & Duke hide money there.
7. Conforming to rules of society
8. Grangerford boy Huck's age
9. Narrator
10. Jim's relationship to Miss Watson
11. ___ Scott
12. Widow Douglas thinks Huck should get this at school.
13. Theme relating to outdoors
14. Leads the mob against Col. Sherburn
15. Solomon, for example
16. Pledge

A=	B=	C=	D=
E=	F=	G=	H=
I=	J=	K=	L=
M=	N=	O=	P=

Huck Finn Magic Squares 3 Answer Key

Match the definition with the vocabulary word. Put your answers in the magic squares below. When your answers are correct, all columns and rows will add to the same number.

A. CIVILIZED
B. WALTER
C. MATTRESS
D. SLAVE
E. HARKNESS
F. BOGGS
G. KING
H. TURNER
I. EDUCATION
J. BUCK
K. HUCK
L. RELIGION
M. CLEMENS
N. NATURE
O. TWAIN
P. OATH

1. A.K.A. Twain
2. Col. Sherburn shot him.
3. Packard & Bill plot to kill him.
4. Author Mark ___
5. Widow Douglas thinks Huck should get this at church.
6. King & Duke hide money there.
7. Conforming to rules of society
8. Grangerford boy Huck's age
9. Narrator
10. Jim's relationship to Miss Watson
11. ___ Scott
12. Widow Douglas thinks Huck should get this at school.
13. Theme relating to outdoors
14. Leads the mob against Col. Sherburn
15. Solomon, for example
16. Pledge

A=7	B=11	C=6	D=10
E=14	F=2	G=15	H=3
I=12	J=8	K=9	L=5
M=1	N=13	O=4	P=16

Huck Finn Magic Squares 4

Match the definition with the vocabulary word. Put your answers in the magic squares below. When your answers are correct, all columns and rows will add to the same number.

A. SILAS
B. FISHING
C. HUCK
D. SALLY
E. BUCK
F. HAIRBALL
G. EDUCATION
H. CLEMENS
I. HARNEY
J. HARKNESS
K. LOFTUS
L. KING
M. BOGGS
N. CABIN
O. RAFT
P. PAP

1. A.K.A. Twain
2. Col. Sherburn shot him.
3. Huck's hook and line pastime
4. Huck visits her in town, dressed as a girl.
5. Leads the mob against Col. Sherburn
6. Narrator
7. Mr. Finn to Huck
8. Grangerford boy Huck's age
9. Huck's river transportation
10. The ___ Oracle
11. Buck shot at this Shepherdson.
12. Mrs. Phelps; Tom's aunt
13. Mr. Phelps
14. Solomon, for example
15. Widow Douglas thinks Huck should get this at school.
16. Huck and Jim found a dead man in one.

A= 13	B= 3	C= 6	D= 12
E= 8	F= 10	G= 15	H= 1
I= 11	J= 5	K= 4	L= 14
M= 2	N= 16	O= 9	P= 7

Huck Finn Magic Squares 4 Answer Key

Match the definition with the vocabulary word. Put your answers in the magic squares below. When your answers are correct, all columns and rows will add to the same number.

A. SILAS
B. FISHING
C. HUCK
D. SALLY
E. BUCK
F. HAIRBALL
G. EDUCATION
H. CLEMENS
I. HARNEY
J. HARKNESS
K. LOFTUS
L. KING
M. BOGGS
N. CABIN
O. RAFT
P. PAP

1. A.K.A. Twain
2. Col. Sherburn shot him.
3. Huck's hook and line pastime
4. Huck visits her in town, dressed as a girl.
5. Leads the mob against Col. Sherburn
6. Narrator
7. Mr. Finn to Huck
8. Grangerford boy Huck's age
9. Huck's river transportation
10. The ___ Oracle
11. Buck shot at this Shepherdson.
12. Mrs. Phelps; Tom's aunt
13. Mr. Phelps
14. Solomon, for example
15. Widow Douglas thinks Huck should get this at school.
16. Huck and Jim found a dead man in one.

A=13	B=3	C=6	D=12
E=8	F=10	G=15	H=1
I=11	J=5	K=4	L=14
M=2	N=16	O=9	P=7

Huck Finn Word Search 1

Words are placed backwards, forward, diagonally, up and down. Clues listed below can help you find the words. Circle the hidden vocabulary words in the maze.

```
S T A O B R E V I R I S L A N D F E F L
F A Q L E E M G R A N G E R F O R D S Y
R C L T P L I M Z N Y D L F F D T U S F
Y H L L D I S A V T G E D C T M X C Y J
V A A J Y G S T Y G D Z Q W H T L A J G
W N B B V I O T N V S I J M A C O T B K
P N R G C O U R I R K L W D T V F I O T
M I I H G N R E A W D I A Z C S T O G Z
W B A D W D I S W M F V N V H W U N G H
A A H M R R P S T W H I S K E Y S N S J
T L Q O Q L N F N U B C S S R F C A E D
S F G D R E A D C A R K F H S T R R S G
O Y D E M R X S C K K N Z C I A M W O D
N W Y E N R A H I Y H E E N H N T O M R
W A L R S L K N Q L T R N R I H G D R F
I C T F G C G X Q L A F W F H B L I Q B
L Q P U J F A P J O O S F J Y U U W Y J
K M A R R B N P D P Z O R I K S C C W Y
S Z P T T E G X E K C U L M H O G K K Q
```

A.K.A. Twain (7)
Author Mark ___ (5)
Buck shot at this Shepherdson. (6)
Col. Sherburn shot him. (5)
Conforming to rules of society (9)
Dead Peter's last name (5)
Grangerford boy Huck's age (4)
Hannibal's state (8)
He told Huck many superstitions. (3)
Huck and Jim found a dead man in one. (5)
Huck hides money there. (6)
Huck uses the blood of one to stage his own death. (3)
Huck visits her in town, dressed as a girl. (6)
Huck's dreamer friend (3)
Huck's girl name (5)
Huck's hook and line pastime (7)
Huck's river transportation (4)
I Discover ___ And The Bulrushers (5)
It can be bad or good: fate (4)
Jackson's ___ (6)
Jim's relationship to Miss Watson (5)
King & Duke hide money there. (8)
Marital status of the Douglas woman (5)
Mr. Finn to Huck (3)
Mr. Phelps (5)

Mrs. Phelps; Tom's aunt (5)
Narrator (4)
One bit Jim. (5)
Opposite of slavery (7)
Packard & Bill plot to kill him. (6)
Pap's drink (7)
Pledge (4)
Sister to Widow Douglas (6)
Solomon, for example (4)
The ___ Oracle (8)
The judge (8)
Theme relating to outdoors (6)
They feud with the Shepherdsons. (12)
They transported goods and people on the Mississippi. (10)
Tom Sawyer was the leader of a ___ of boys. (4)
Tom and Huck help Jim do this. (6)
Tom's aunt and guardian (5)
Twain's hometown (8)
Widow Douglas thinks Huck should get this at church. (8)
Widow Douglas thinks Huck should get this at school. (9)
___ Scott (6)

Huck Finn Word Search 1 Answer Key

Words are placed backwards, forward, diagonally, up and down. Clues listed below can help you find the words. Circle the hidden vocabulary words in the maze.

A.K.A. Twain (7)
Author Mark ___ (5)
Buck shot at this Shepherdson. (6)
Col. Sherburn shot him. (5)
Conforming to rules of society (9)
Dead Peter's last name (5)
Grangerford boy Huck's age (4)
Hannibal's state (8)
He told Huck many superstitions. (3)
Huck and Jim found a dead man in one. (5)
Huck hides money there. (6)
Huck uses the blood of one to stage his own death. (3)
Huck visits her in town, dressed as a girl. (6)
Huck's dreamer friend (3)
Huck's girl name (5)
Huck's hook and line pastime (7)
Huck's river transportation (4)
I Discover ___ And The Bulrushers (5)
It can be bad or good: fate (4)
Jackson's ___ (6)
Jim's relationship to Miss Watson (5)
King & Duke hide money there. (8)
Marital status of the Douglas woman (5)
Mr. Finn to Huck (3)
Mr. Phelps (5)

Mrs. Phelps; Tom's aunt (5)
Narrator (4)
One bit Jim. (5)
Opposite of slavery (7)
Packard & Bill plot to kill him. (6)
Pap's drink (7)
Pledge (4)
Sister to Widow Douglas (6)
Solomon, for example (4)
The ___ Oracle (8)
The judge (8)
Theme relating to outdoors (6)
They feud with the Shepherdsons. (12)
They transported goods and people on the Mississippi. (10)
Tom Sawyer was the leader of a ___ of boys. (4)
Tom and Huck help Jim do this. (6)
Tom's aunt and guardian (5)
Twain's hometown (8)
Widow Douglas thinks Huck should get this at church. (8)
Widow Douglas thinks Huck should get this at school. (9)
___ Scott (6)

Huck Finn Word Search 2

Words are placed backwards, forward, diagonally, up and down. Clues listed below can help you find the words. Circle the hidden vocabulary words in the maze.

```
G R A N G E R F O R D S J I M W H Y M K
S M E O S R H W V W K H B O O H L U K S
N A D S R T A K H L Q N S D T L B T C W
R T U T R S R S I I S E I A A B U C K K
G T C A H T N W W Y S W O S L A V E D R
Y R A W X A E L F G E K L W I M X P M B
V E T V K O Y G G V N H E P J L J A X F
N S I E L B N O V F K I A Y N F A C M K
R S O R O B T F A R S T I I T M S X P
L R N U F E C P H U A W A S R O Z E G M
F C L T T V D D O A H W H L T B D D O Y
C K V A U I F S V K T I K A Y F A D L Y
T X V N S R S P G F N C S N E M E L C J
S U C Z K I R N G G U O H D T E O K L J
G G R Q M E I P B L F F L E R P B M C C
D A T N T K D A V F Z F X F R S A R A H
P N H L E R H P C I V I L I Z E D V B D
C G A O M R L P H A N N I B A L S W I S
P W Y N G M J R E L I G I O N S X V N W
```

A.K.A. Twain (7)
Author Mark ___ (5)
Buck shot at this Shepherdson. (6)
Col. Sherburn shot him. (5)
Conforming to rules of society (9)
Dead Peter's last name (5)
Grangerford boy Huck's age (4)
Hannibal's state (8)
He told Huck many superstitions. (3)
Huck and Jim found a dead man in one. (5)
Huck hides money there. (6)
Huck uses the blood of one to stage his own death. (3)
Huck visits her in town, dressed as a girl. (6)
Huck's dreamer friend (3)
Huck's girl name (5)
Huck's hook and line pastime (7)
Huck's river transportation (4)
I Discover ___ And The Bulrushers (5)
It can be bad or good: fate (4)
Jackson's ___ (6)
Jim's relationship to Miss Watson (5)
King & Duke hide money there. (8)
Leads the mob against Col. Sherburn (8)
Marital status of the Douglas woman (5)
Mr. Finn to Huck (3)

Mr. Phelps (5)
Mrs. Phelps; Tom's aunt (5)
Narrator (4)
One bit Jim. (5)
Opposite of slavery (7)
Packard & Bill plot to kill him. (6)
Pap's drink (7)
Pledge (4)
Sister to Widow Douglas (6)
Solomon, for example (4)
The ___ Oracle (8)
The judge (8)
Theme relating to outdoors (6)
They feud with the Shepherdsons. (12)
They transported goods and people on the Mississippi. (10)
Tom Sawyer was the leader of a ___ of boys. (4)
Tom and Huck help Jim do this. (6)
Tom's aunt and guardian (5)
Twain's hometown (8)
Widow Douglas thinks Huck should get this at church. (8)
Widow Douglas thinks Huck should get this at school. (9)
___ Scott (6)

Huck Finn Word Search 2 Answer Key

Words are placed backwards, forward, diagonally, up and down. Clues listed below can help you find the words. Circle the hidden vocabulary words in the maze.

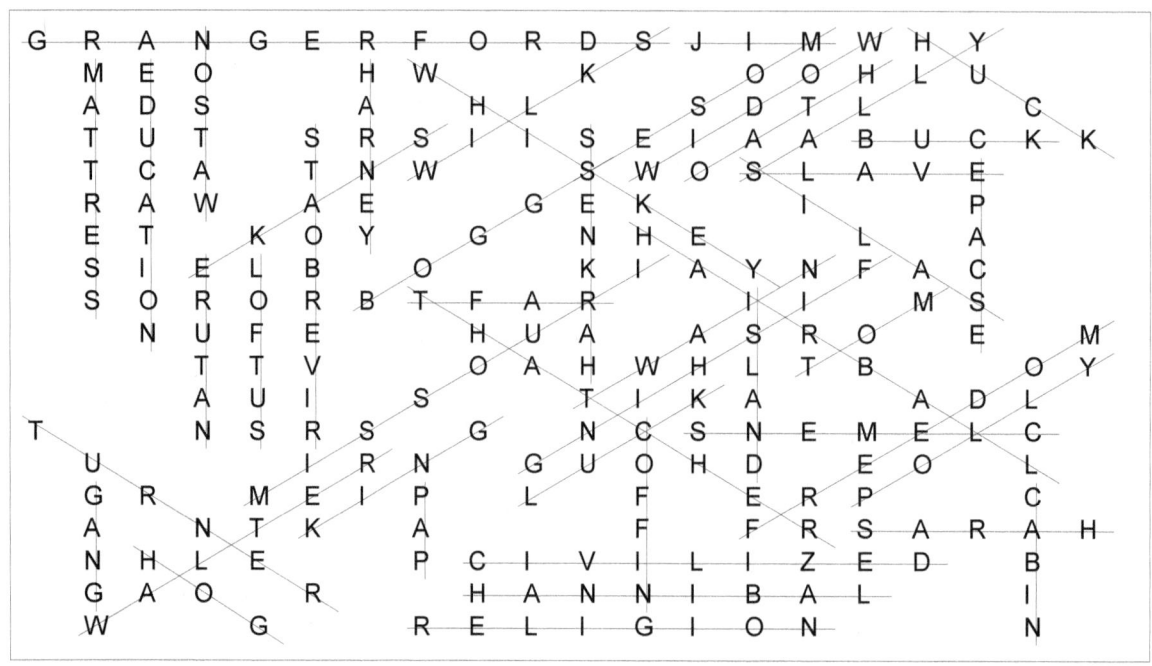

A.K.A. Twain (7)
Author Mark ___ (5)
Buck shot at this Shepherdson. (6)
Col. Sherburn shot him. (5)
Conforming to rules of society (9)
Dead Peter's last name (5)
Grangerford boy Huck's age (4)
Hannibal's state (8)
He told Huck many superstitions. (3)
Huck and Jim found a dead man in one. (5)
Huck hides money there. (6)
Huck uses the blood of one to stage his own death. (3)
Huck visits her in town, dressed as a girl. (6)
Huck's dreamer friend (3)
Huck's girl name (5)
Huck's hook and line pastime (7)
Huck's river transportation (4)
I Discover ___ And The Bulrushers (5)
It can be bad or good: fate (4)
Jackson's ___ (6)
Jim's relationship to Miss Watson (5)
King & Duke hide money there. (8)
Leads the mob against Col. Sherburn (8)
Marital status of the Douglas woman (5)
Mr. Finn to Huck (3)

Mr. Phelps (5)
Mrs. Phelps; Tom's aunt (5)
Narrator (4)
One bit Jim. (5)
Opposite of slavery (7)
Packard & Bill plot to kill him. (6)
Pap's drink (7)
Pledge (4)
Sister to Widow Douglas (6)
Solomon, for example (4)
The ___ Oracle (8)
The judge (8)
Theme relating to outdoors (6)
They feud with the Shepherdsons. (12)
They transported goods and people on the Mississippi. (10)
Tom Sawyer was the leader of a ___ of boys. (4)
Tom and Huck help Jim do this. (6)
Tom's aunt and guardian (5)
Twain's hometown (8)
Widow Douglas thinks Huck should get this at church. (8)
Widow Douglas thinks Huck should get this at school. (9)
___ Scott (6)

Huck Finn Word Search 3

Words are placed backwards, forward, diagonally, up and down. Words listed below are included in the maze. Circle the hidden vocabulary words in the maze.

```
W M I S S I S S I P P I G B G H U C K J
A I H A N N I B A L N N C N O M V C F J
T H D Y Y N J M Z V I G A O H Z U Z Z Z
S A R O K N L G F H T G M B F L T J M W
O I K F W Q S G S N P O L L Y F W L K C
N R L M Y N N I C S D Y M E V H I C N X
L B T X E I F Q K E E S K X W N U N A R
X A E M K H G S E N K S S G J B B D T J
Z L E D V N U R R L I C A R Q W O Y U W
T L X C U T F A I H H I R G N A G N R L
C T X N F C H W W N S V A Q O L G R E D
G N G O W V A A Y T J I H I I T S E X D
J J L B E X C T T V X L D R G E S N V R
M T J H D S L S I C Q I K U I R P R S C
C T W T C T C L P O H Z H O L S K U N R
I S L A N D H A R K N E S S E R T T A M
D F B O I P P V P M J D R S R R L F K F
H I Y H M N Z E N E M S O I T L T D E Z
N J I M S I L A S Y P M D M S A L L Y L
```

BOGGS	GANG	LOFTUS	RAFT	TWAIN
BUCK	HAIRBALL	LUCK	RELIGION	WALTER
CABIN	HANNIBAL	MATTRESS	SALLY	WATSON
CIVILIZED	HARKNESS	MISSISSIPPI	SARAH	WHISKEY
CLEMENS	HARNEY	MISSOURI	SILAS	WIDOW
COFFIN	HOG	MOSES	SLAVE	WILKS
EDUCATION	HUCK	NATURE	SNAKE	
ESCAPE	ISLAND	OATH	THATCHER	
FISHING	JIM	PAP	TOM	
FREEDOM	KING	POLLY	TURNER	

Huck Finn Word Search 3 Answer Key

Words are placed backwards, forward, diagonally, up and down. Words listed below are included in the maze. Circle the hidden vocabulary words in the maze.

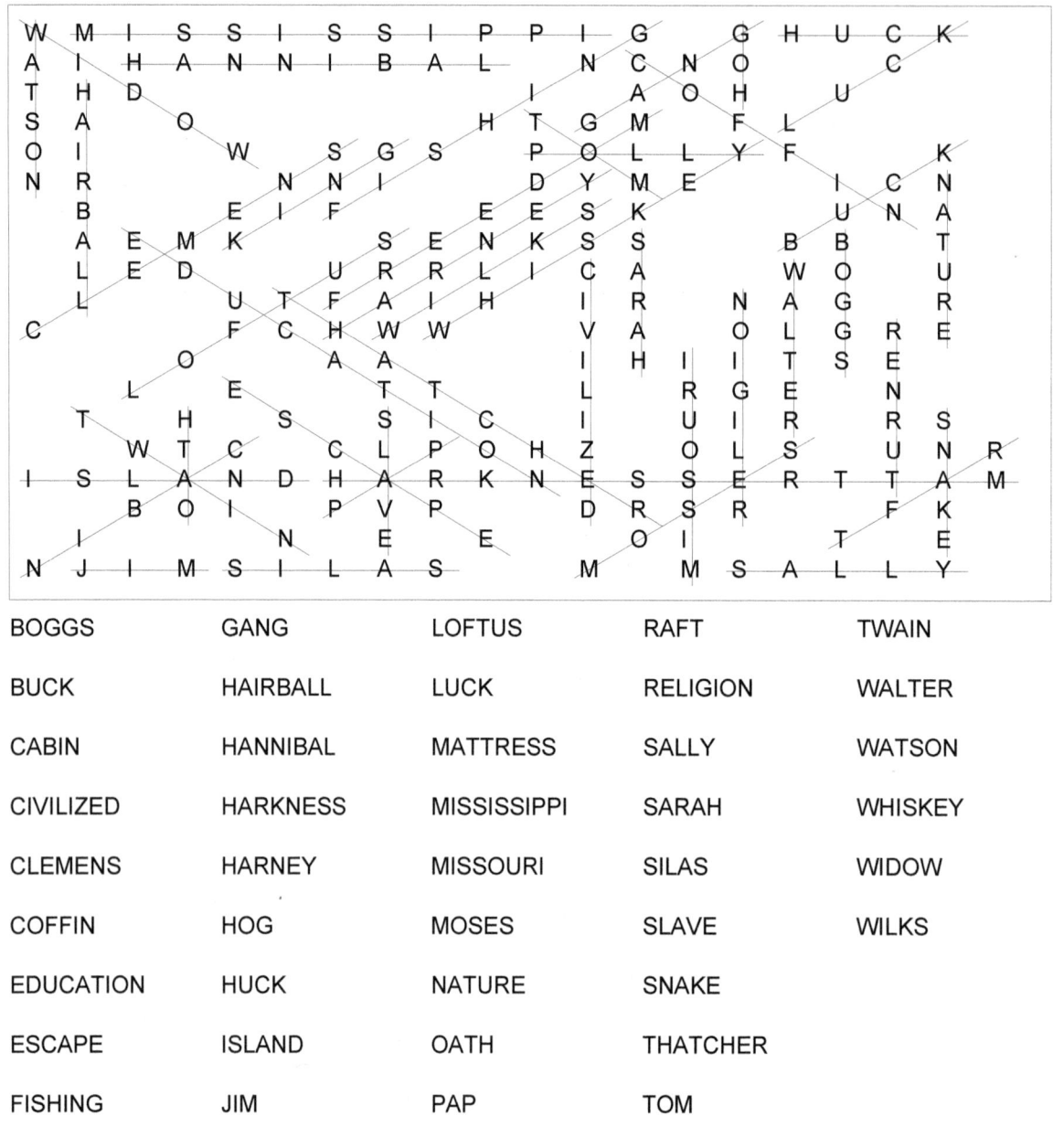

BOGGS	GANG	LOFTUS	RAFT	TWAIN
BUCK	HAIRBALL	LUCK	RELIGION	WALTER
CABIN	HANNIBAL	MATTRESS	SALLY	WATSON
CIVILIZED	HARKNESS	MISSISSIPPI	SARAH	WHISKEY
CLEMENS	HARNEY	MISSOURI	SILAS	WIDOW
COFFIN	HOG	MOSES	SLAVE	WILKS
EDUCATION	HUCK	NATURE	SNAKE	
ESCAPE	ISLAND	OATH	THATCHER	
FISHING	JIM	PAP	TOM	
FREEDOM	KING	POLLY	TURNER	

Huck Finn Word Search 4

Words are placed backwards, forward, diagonally, up and down. Words listed below are included in the maze. Circle the hidden vocabulary words in the maze.

```
T P O L L Y E D U C A T I O N L S M H X
R U I R U O S S I M C N R N N N O A A D
I A R H C N X F Y S S C P K E D M T R V
V W F N K W H I S K E Y P M E Y K T K Z
E I R T E N O S T A W X E E E D N R N G
R D E E Q R G H H S K L R N Q I A E E F
B O L Z S G C I N A C F R V A K T S S S
O W I H O C M N J Q N A G W D X U S S E
A O G B N I A G H V H N T V J X R R V T
T A I P W P R P Y O F T I M T Z E A N B
S T O L K P P J E H G H H B S N L D B J
T H N F S I C O F F I N J A A S L R W T
C Q S W U S S X W W C N P R T L B B A J
A K A N T S N R I G C S B L A C Z Q L Q
B D L M F I A L S K I C W B F J H X T P
I D L G O S K W L L G V R G Z F K E E L
N N Y M L S E P A P K I N G K C U H R P
N T I O S I E S N T A A C P U Q G Y B L
N J H T R M V S D H G B Z B S A R A H X
```

BOGGS	HAIRBALL	LUCK	RELIGION	TWAIN
BUCK	HANNIBAL	MATTRESS	RIVERBOATS	WALTER
CABIN	HARKNESS	MISSISSIPPI	SALLY	WATSON
CLEMENS	HARNEY	MISSOURI	SARAH	WHISKEY
COFFIN	HOG	MOSES	SILAS	WIDOW
EDUCATION	HUCK	NATURE	SLAVE	WILKS
ESCAPE	ISLAND	OATH	SNAKE	
FISHING	JIM	PAP	THATCHER	
FREEDOM	KING	POLLY	TOM	
GANG	LOFTUS	RAFT	TURNER	

Huck Finn Word Search 4 Answer Key

Words are placed backwards, forward, diagonally, up and down. Words listed below are included in the maze. Circle the hidden vocabulary words in the maze.

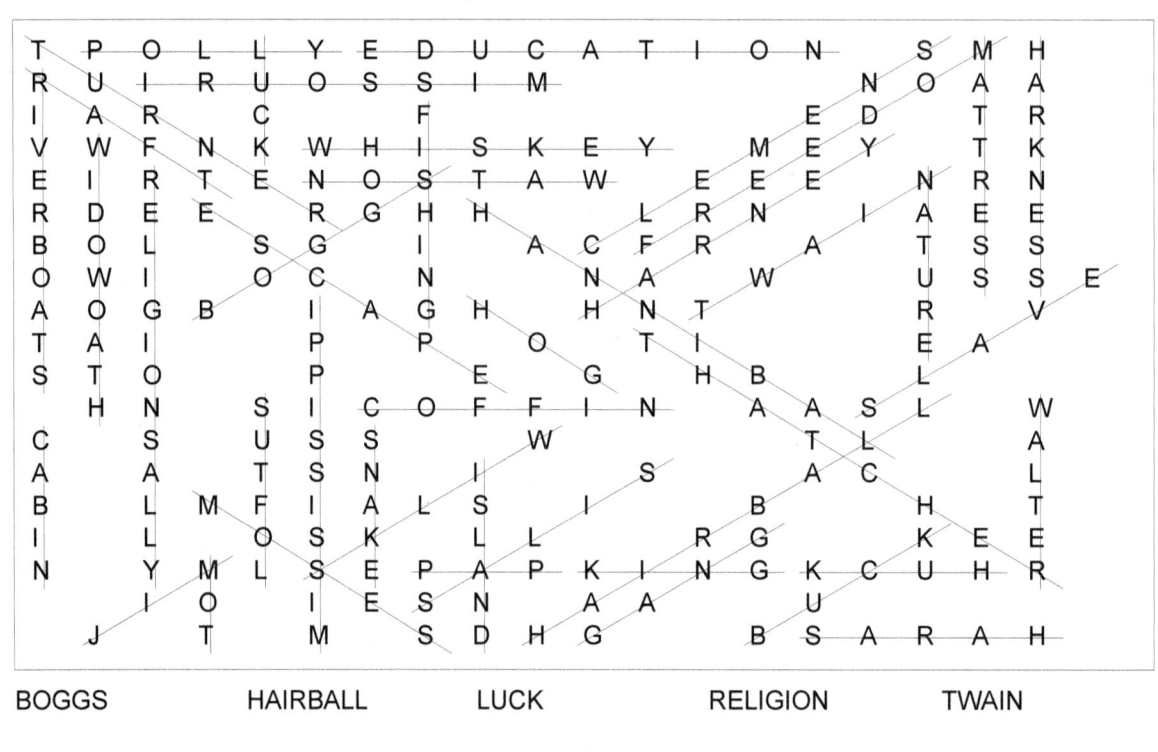

BOGGS	HAIRBALL	LUCK	RELIGION	TWAIN
BUCK	HANNIBAL	MATTRESS	RIVERBOATS	WALTER
CABIN	HARKNESS	MISSISSIPPI	SALLY	WATSON
CLEMENS	HARNEY	MISSOURI	SARAH	WHISKEY
COFFIN	HOG	MOSES	SILAS	WIDOW
EDUCATION	HUCK	NATURE	SLAVE	WILKS
ESCAPE	ISLAND	OATH	SNAKE	
FISHING	JIM	PAP	THATCHER	
FREEDOM	KING	POLLY	TOM	
GANG	LOFTUS	RAFT	TURNER	

Huck Finn Crossword 1

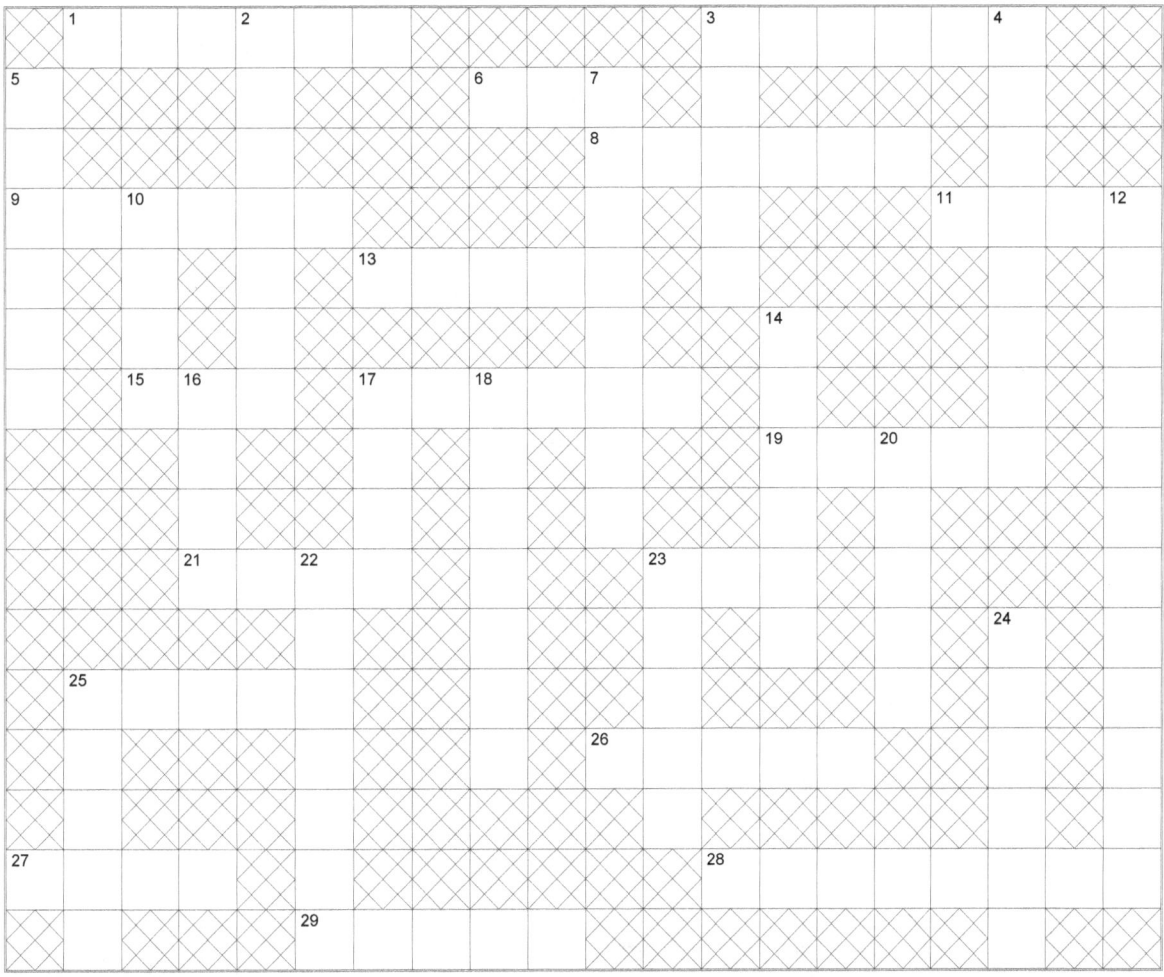

Across
1. Huck hides money there.
3. ___ Scott
6. He told Huck many superstitions.
8. Jackson's ___
9. Packard & Bill plot to kill him.
11. Solomon, for example
13. Mr. Phelps
15. Huck's dreamer friend
17. Huck visits her in town, dressed as a girl.
19. Huck and Jim found a dead man in one.
21. Narrator
23. Mr. Finn to Huck
25. One bit Jim.
26. Jim's relationship to Miss Watson
27. Tom Sawyer was the leader of a ___ of boys.
28. King & Duke hide money there.
29. Mrs. Phelps; Tom's aunt

Down
2. Opposite of slavery
3. Dead Peter's last name
4. Widow Douglas thinks Huck should get this at church.
5. Theme relating to outdoors
7. Hannibal's state
10. Huck's river transportation
12. They feud with the Shepherdsons.
14. Tom and Huck help Jim do this.
16. Pledge
17. It can be bad or good: fate
18. Huck's hook and line pastime
20. Col. Sherburn shot him.
22. A.K.A. Twain
23. Tom's aunt and guardian
24. Buck shot at this Shepherdson.
25. Huck's girl name

Huck Finn Crossword 1 Answer Key

	1 C	O	2 F	F	I	N			3 W	A	L	T	E	4 R	
5 N			R				6 J	7 M	I				E	
A			E				8 I	S	L	A	N	D		
9 T	10 U	R	N	E	R		S	K			11 K	I	N	12 G
U	A		D		13 S	I	L	A	S			G		R
R	F		O				O	14 E			I		A
E	15 T	16 O	M	17 L	18 F	T	U	S				O	N
		A		U		I		R	19 C	20 B	I	N		G
		T		C		S		I	A		O			E
	21 H	U	22 C	K		H		23 P	A	P		G		R
		L		I				O	E			24 H	F
25 S	N	A	K	E		N		L			S	A	O
	A		M			26 G	S	L	A	V	E		R	R
	R		E				Y					N	D
27 G	A	N	G	N			28 M	A	T	T	R	E	S	S
	H		29 S	A	L	L	Y						Y	

Across
1. Huck hides money there.
3. ___ Scott
6. He told Huck many superstitions.
8. Jackson's ___
9. Packard & Bill plot to kill him.
11. Solomon, for example
13. Mr. Phelps
15. Huck's dreamer friend
17. Huck visits her in town, dressed as a girl.
19. Huck and Jim found a dead man in one.
21. Narrator
23. Mr. Finn to Huck
25. One bit Jim.
26. Jim's relationship to Miss Watson
27. Tom Sawyer was the leader of a ___ of boys.
28. King & Duke hide money there.
29. Mrs. Phelps; Tom's aunt

Down
2. Opposite of slavery
3. Dead Peter's last name
4. Widow Douglas thinks Huck should get this at church.
5. Theme relating to outdoors
7. Hannibal's state
10. Huck's river transportation
12. They feud with the Shepherdsons.
14. Tom and Huck help Jim do this.
16. Pledge
17. It can be bad or good: fate
18. Huck's hook and line pastime
20. Col. Sherburn shot him.
22. A.K.A. Twain
23. Tom's aunt and guardian
24. Buck shot at this Shepherdson.
25. Huck's girl name

Huck Finn Crossword 2

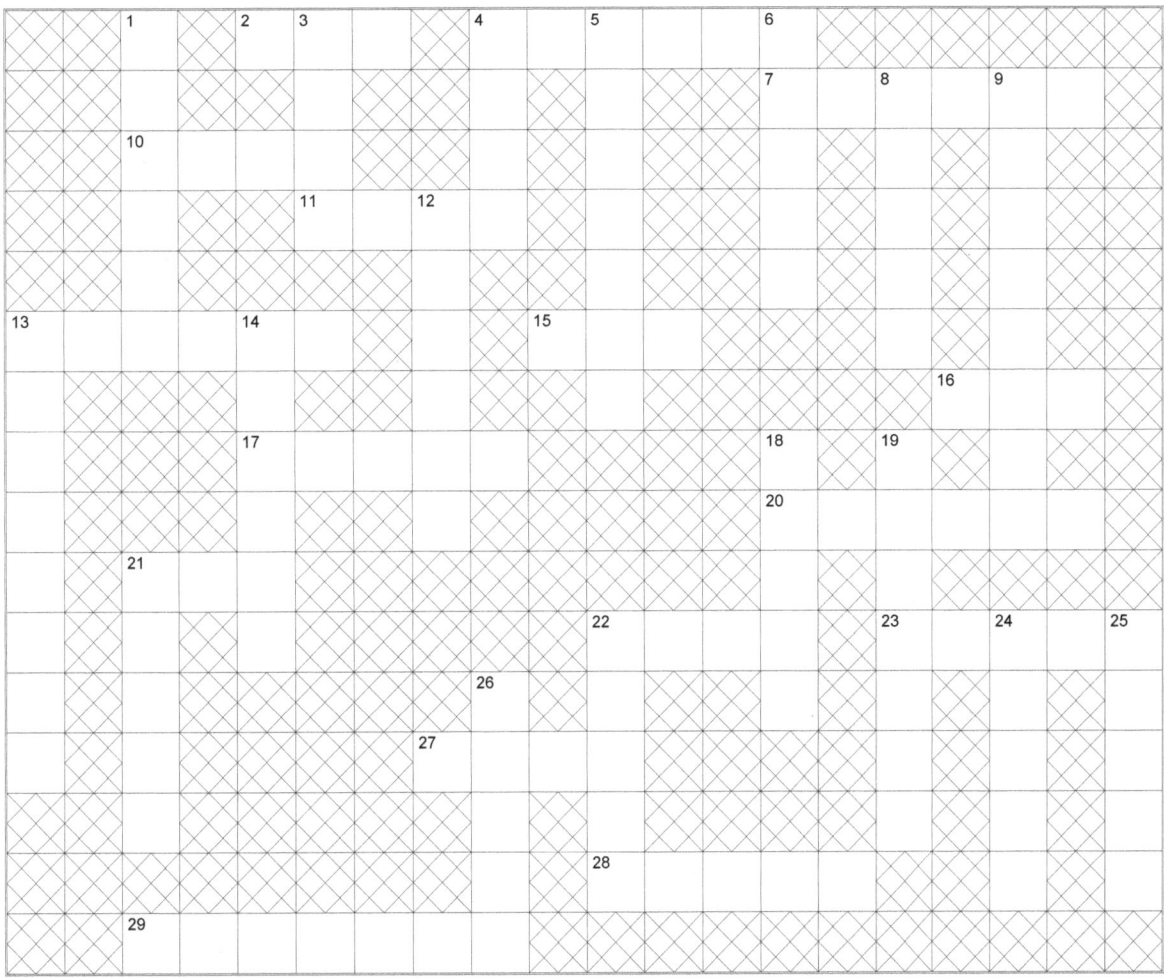

Across
2. Huck's dreamer friend
4. Huck visits her in town, dressed as a girl.
7. Theme relating to outdoors
10. Huck's river transportation
11. Narrator
13. Buck shot at this Shepherdson.
15. Huck uses the blood of one to stage his own death.
16. He told Huck many superstitions.
17. Huck and Jim found a dead man in one.
20. Jackson's ___
21. Mr. Finn to Huck
22. Grangerford boy Huck's age
23. I Discover ___ And The Bulrushers
27. Tom Sawyer was the leader of a ___ of boys.
28. Jim's relationship to Miss Watson
29. Pap's drink

Down
1. Packard & Bill plot to kill him.
3. Pledge
4. It can be bad or good: fate
5. Opposite of slavery
6. One bit Jim.
8. Author Mark ___
9. Widow Douglas thinks Huck should get this at church.
12. Huck hides money there.
13. Twain's hometown
14. Tom and Huck help Jim do this.
18. Dead Peter's last name
19. A.K.A. Twain
21. Tom's aunt and guardian
22. Col. Sherburn shot him.
24. Mr. Phelps
25. Huck's girl name
26. Mrs. Phelps; Tom's aunt

Huck Finn Crossword 2 Answer Key

		1 T		2 T	3 O	M		4 L	O	5 F	T	U	6 S			
		U			A			U		R		7 N	A	8 T	U	9 R	E
		10 R	A	F	T			C		E		A		W		E
		N		11 H	U	12 C	K		E		K		A		L
		E				O		D		E		I		I
13 H	A	R	N	14 E	Y		15 H	O	G			N		G
A				S		F		M				16 J	I	M
N		17 C	A	B	I	N			18 W	19 C	O	
N			A		N			20 I	S	L	A	N	D
I		21 P	A	P				L		E	
B		O		E		22 B	U	C	K		23 M	O	24 S	E	25 S
A		L			26 S	O		S		E		I		A
L		L			27 G	A	N	G		N		L		R
Y				L		G		S		A
				L		28 S	L	A	V	E		S		H
	29 W	H	I	S	K	E	Y

Across
2. Huck's dreamer friend
4. Huck visits her in town, dressed as a girl.
7. Theme relating to outdoors
10. Huck's river transportation
11. Narrator
13. Buck shot at this Shepherdson.
15. Huck uses the blood of one to stage his own death.
16. He told Huck many superstitions.
17. Huck and Jim found a dead man in one.
20. Jackson's ___
21. Mr. Finn to Huck
22. Grangerford boy Huck's age
23. I Discover ___ And The Bulrushers
27. Tom Sawyer was the leader of a ___ of boys.
28. Jim's relationship to Miss Watson
29. Pap's drink

Down
1. Packard & Bill plot to kill him.
3. Pledge
4. It can be bad or good: fate
5. Opposite of slavery
6. One bit Jim.
8. Author Mark ___
9. Widow Douglas thinks Huck should get this at church.
12. Huck hides money there.
13. Twain's hometown
14. Tom and Huck help Jim do this.
18. Dead Peter's last name
19. A.K.A. Twain
21. Tom's aunt and guardian
22. Col. Sherburn shot him.
24. Mr. Phelps
25. Huck's girl name
26. Mrs. Phelps; Tom's aunt

Huck Finn Crossword 3

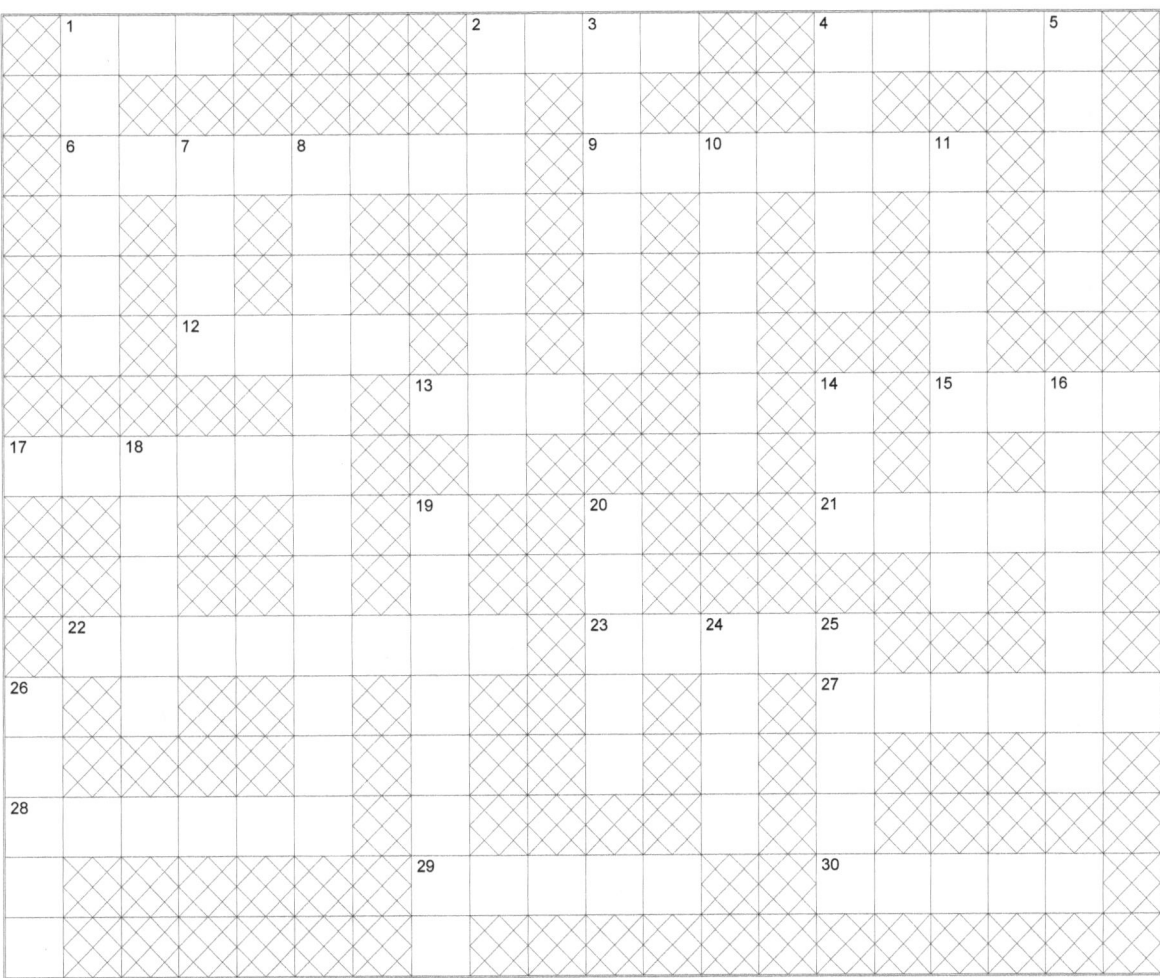

Across
1. Huck's dreamer friend
2. Narrator
4. Dead Peter's last name
6. Widow Douglas thinks Huck should get this at church.
9. Opposite of slavery
12. Solomon, for example
13. Mr. Finn to Huck
15. Huck's river transportation
17. Theme relating to outdoors
21. I Discover ___ And The Bulrushers
22. Hannibal's state
23. Col. Sherburn shot him.
27. Jackson's ___
28. Huck visits her in town, dressed as a girl.
29. Huck's girl name
30. Mrs. Phelps; Tom's aunt

Down
1. Packard & Bill plot to kill him.
2. Twain's hometown
3. Huck hides money there.
4. Marital status of the Douglas woman
5. One bit Jim.
7. It can be bad or good: fate
8. They feud with the Shepherdsons.
10. Tom and Huck help Jim do this.
11. King & Duke hide money there.
14. He told Huck many superstitions.
16. Huck's hook and line pastime
18. Author Mark ___
19. Leads the mob against Col. Sherburn
20. Huck and Jim found a dead man in one.
24. Tom Sawyer was the leader of a ___ of boys.
25. Mr. Phelps
26. Tom's aunt and guardian

Huck Finn Crossword 3 Answer Key

	1 T	O	M		2 H	3 C	K		4 W	I	L	K	5 S
	U				A	O			I				N
	6 R	7 E	8 L	I	G	I	O	N	9 F	10 R	E	E	11 D	O	M	A
	N	U	R		N	F			S		O		A	K
	E	C	A		I	I			C		W		T	E
	R	12 K	I	N	G	B			N		A		T	
			G	13 P	A	P			14 P	15 R	A	16 F	T
17 N	18 A	T	U	R	E		L			E		I	E		I
		W			R		19 H		20 C		21 M	O	S	E	S
		A			F		A		A			S		H
	22 M	I	S	S	O	U	R	I	23 B	24 O	25 G	G	S		I
26 P		N			R		K		I	A	27 I	S	L	A	N	D
O					D		N		N	N	L				G
28 L	O	F	T	U	S		E			G	A		
L					29 S	A	R	A	H		30 S	A	L	L	Y
Y					S							

Across
1. Huck's dreamer friend
2. Narrator
4. Dead Peter's last name
6. Widow Douglas thinks Huck should get this at church.
9. Opposite of slavery
12. Solomon, for example
13. Mr. Finn to Huck
15. Huck's river transportation
17. Theme relating to outdoors
21. I Discover ___ And The Bulrushers
22. Hannibal's state
23. Col. Sherburn shot him.
27. Jackson's ___
28. Huck visits her in town, dressed as a girl.
29. Huck's girl name
30. Mrs. Phelps; Tom's aunt

Down
1. Packard & Bill plot to kill him.
2. Twain's hometown
3. Huck hides money there.
4. Marital status of the Douglas woman
5. One bit Jim.
7. It can be bad or good: fate
8. They feud with the Shepherdsons.
10. Tom and Huck help Jim do this.
11. King & Duke hide money there.
14. He told Huck many superstitions.
16. Huck's hook and line pastime
18. Author Mark ___
19. Leads the mob against Col. Sherburn
20. Huck and Jim found a dead man in one.
24. Tom Sawyer was the leader of a ___ of boys.
25. Mr. Phelps
26. Tom's aunt and guardian

Huck Finn Crossword 4

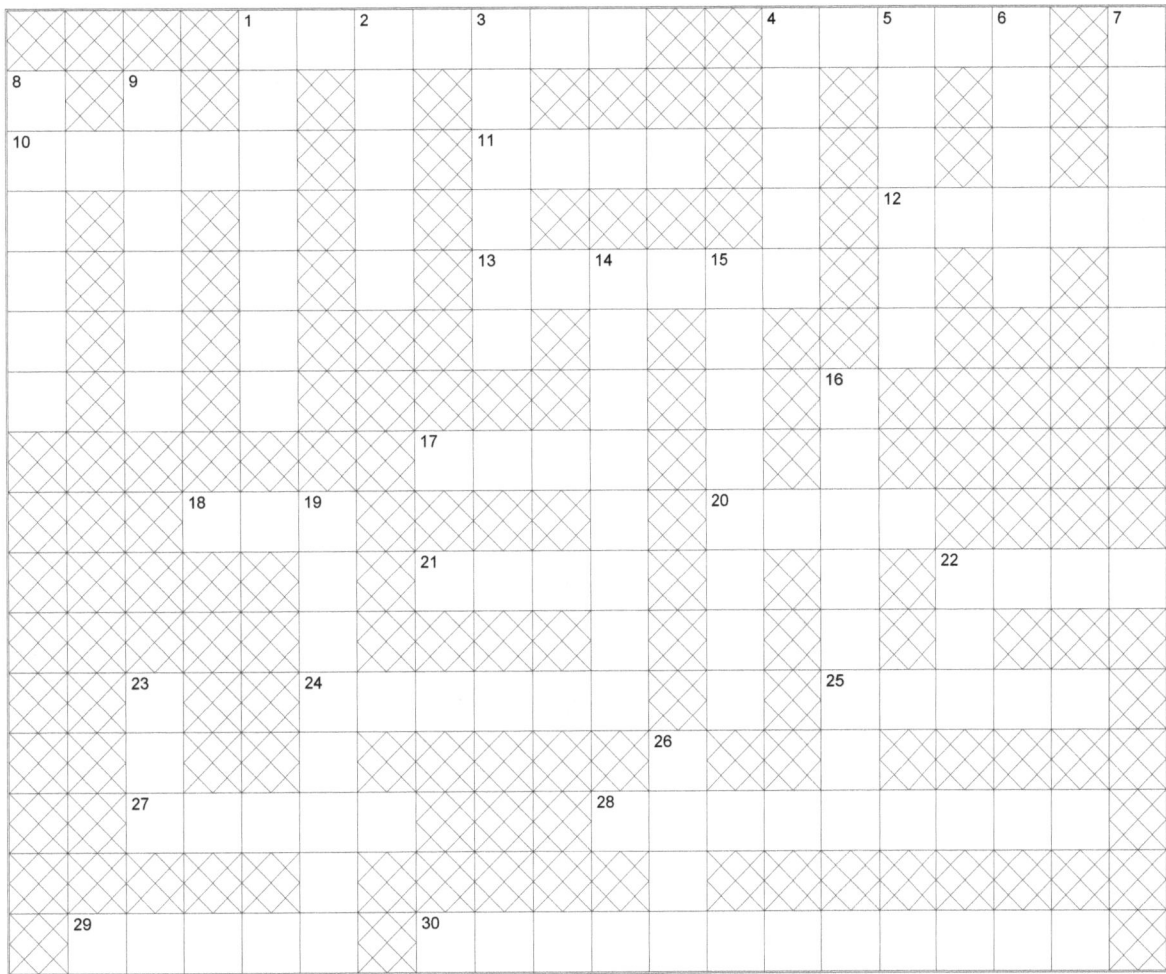

Across
1. Huck's hook and line pastime
4. Mr. Phelps
10. One bit Jim.
11. It can be bad or good: fate
12. Author Mark ___
13. Theme relating to outdoors
17. Huck's river transportation
18. He told Huck many superstitions.
20. Tom Sawyer was the leader of a ___ of boys.
21. Pledge
22. Narrator
24. Packard & Bill plot to kill him.
25. Col. Sherburn shot him.
27. I Discover ___ And The Bulrushers
28. Conforming to rules of society
29. Dead Peter's last name
30. They feud with the Shepherdsons.

Down
1. Opposite of slavery
2. Mrs. Phelps; Tom's aunt
3. Jackson's ___
4. Jim's relationship to Miss Watson
5. Huck visits her in town, dressed as a girl.
6. Huck's girl name
7. Buck shot at this Shepherdson.
8. Tom and Huck help Jim do this.
9. ___ Scott
14. The judge
15. Widow Douglas thinks Huck should get this at church.
16. Twain's hometown
19. King & Duke hide money there.
22. Huck uses the blood of one to stage his own death.
23. Huck's dreamer friend
26. Solomon, for example

Huck Finn Crossword 4 Answer Key

Across
1. Huck's hook and line pastime
4. Mr. Phelps
10. One bit Jim.
11. It can be bad or good: fate
12. Author Mark ___
13. Theme relating to outdoors
17. Huck's river transportation
18. He told Huck many superstitions.
20. Tom Sawyer was the leader of a ___ of boys.
21. Pledge
22. Narrator
24. Packard & Bill plot to kill him.
25. Col. Sherburn shot him.
27. I Discover ___ And The Bulrushers
28. Conforming to rules of society
29. Dead Peter's last name
30. They feud with the Shepherdsons.

Down
1. Opposite of slavery
2. Mrs. Phelps; Tom's aunt
3. Jackson's ___
4. Jim's relationship to Miss Watson
5. Huck visits her in town, dressed as a girl.
6. Huck's girl name
7. Buck shot at this Shepherdson.
8. Tom and Huck help Jim do this.
9. ___ Scott
14. The judge
15. Widow Douglas thinks Huck should get this at church.
16. Twain's hometown
19. King & Duke hide money there.
22. Huck uses the blood of one to stage his own death.
23. Huck's dreamer friend
26. Solomon, for example

Huck Finn

BUCK	TOM	TURNER	CABIN	GRANGERFORDS
WIDOW	SNAKE	BOGGS	SARAH	PAP
RIVERBOATS	SILAS	FREE SPACE	JIM	NATURE
LOFTUS	OATH	HUCK	HANNIBAL	HAIRBALL
HARNEY	WALTER	ESCAPE	WHISKEY	POLLY

Huck Finn

RELIGION	SALLY	GANG	COFFIN	MATTRESS
SLAVE	MOSES	KING	HOG	ISLAND
LUCK	MISSOURI	FREE SPACE	EDUCATION	CLEMENS
RAFT	TWAIN	WATSON	FISHING	HARKNESS
THATCHER	WILKS	CIVILIZED	POLLY	WHISKEY

Huck Finn

SILAS	BUCK	CIVILIZED	FREEDOM	MISSOURI
ESCAPE	COFFIN	FISHING	GANG	MATTRESS
RAFT	HUCK	FREE SPACE	MOSES	HARNEY
GRANGERFORDS	NATURE	SNAKE	CABIN	EDUCATION
KING	RELIGION	WIDOW	TWAIN	WALTER

Huck Finn

RIVERBOATS	WILKS	MISSISSIPPI	BOGGS	ISLAND
PAP	HARKNESS	POLLY	TURNER	TOM
JIM	SARAH	FREE SPACE	WHISKEY	WATSON
CLEMENS	HAIRBALL	SALLY	LUCK	SLAVE
HOG	THATCHER	LOFTUS	WALTER	TWAIN

Huck Finn

MOSES	ISLAND	OATH	ESCAPE	TOM
GANG	THATCHER	SILAS	WILKS	RAFT
WIDOW	HANNIBAL	FREE SPACE	POLLY	GRANGERFORDS
FISHING	JIM	LUCK	SARAH	RIVERBOATS
HUCK	WALTER	PAP	SLAVE	MISSISSIPPI

Huck Finn

EDUCATION	BOGGS	HAIRBALL	COFFIN	CLEMENS
HARKNESS	MATTRESS	BUCK	KING	SNAKE
MISSOURI	CABIN	FREE SPACE	HOG	NATURE
LOFTUS	CIVILIZED	WATSON	FREEDOM	WHISKEY
TWAIN	HARNEY	RELIGION	MISSISSIPPI	SLAVE

Huck Finn

EDUCATION	ISLAND	OATH	TURNER	RELIGION
GRANGERFORDS	CLEMENS	NATURE	CIVILIZED	WATSON
TOM	JIM	FREE SPACE	PAP	FISHING
COFFIN	TWAIN	HAIRBALL	BUCK	SLAVE
MATTRESS	SALLY	RIVERBOATS	BOGGS	KING

Huck Finn

HARNEY	GANG	HUCK	HANNIBAL	ESCAPE
MISSISSIPPI	FREEDOM	SILAS	POLLY	CABIN
MISSOURI	RAFT	FREE SPACE	WIDOW	SARAH
HOG	HARKNESS	LUCK	WHISKEY	MOSES
WILKS	WALTER	LOFTUS	KING	BOGGS

Huck Finn

BOGGS	ISLAND	COFFIN	MISSOURI	KING
POLLY	ESCAPE	NATURE	HAIRBALL	GRANGERFORDS
SILAS	LOFTUS	FREE SPACE	FREEDOM	FISHING
WIDOW	TOM	WILKS	HUCK	HARNEY
RIVERBOATS	SALLY	HOG	SARAH	JIM

Huck Finn

CLEMENS	EDUCATION	RELIGION	CIVILIZED	PAP
MATTRESS	WHISKEY	HARKNESS	SNAKE	WATSON
RAFT	MOSES	FREE SPACE	BUCK	LUCK
MISSISSIPPI	TWAIN	CABIN	OATH	WALTER
HANNIBAL	TURNER	SLAVE	JIM	SARAH

Huck Finn

WHISKEY	GANG	OATH	LOFTUS	ISLAND
EDUCATION	BUCK	CLEMENS	MOSES	GRANGERFORDS
KING	WALTER	FREE SPACE	MISSISSIPPI	SILAS
WATSON	MATTRESS	RELIGION	TWAIN	PAP
MISSOURI	CABIN	BOGGS	SLAVE	HARNEY

Huck Finn

RAFT	CIVILIZED	JIM	ESCAPE	NATURE
POLLY	HAIRBALL	WIDOW	RIVERBOATS	THATCHER
HOG	WILKS	FREE SPACE	SALLY	SARAH
FREEDOM	COFFIN	TURNER	HUCK	SNAKE
FISHING	LUCK	HARKNESS	HARNEY	SLAVE

Huck Finn

TWAIN	SNAKE	LOFTUS	BOGGS	KING
TOM	WILKS	HOG	FISHING	MISSISSIPPI
RELIGION	HARKNESS	FREE SPACE	CLEMENS	JIM
HARNEY	NATURE	WATSON	PAP	FREEDOM
WHISKEY	CABIN	WALTER	OATH	EDUCATION

Huck Finn

SLAVE	THATCHER	SILAS	BUCK	GRANGERFORDS
MATTRESS	MISSOURI	WIDOW	ESCAPE	CIVILIZED
MOSES	GANG	FREE SPACE	POLLY	RIVERBOATS
HAIRBALL	SARAH	COFFIN	TURNER	HUCK
ISLAND	HANNIBAL	RAFT	EDUCATION	OATH

Huck Finn

NATURE	SLAVE	WHISKEY	MATTRESS	TOM
JIM	HUCK	EDUCATION	WATSON	LUCK
KING	TURNER	FREE SPACE	RELIGION	POLLY
WILKS	HAIRBALL	WALTER	ISLAND	GANG
CABIN	SALLY	TWAIN	PAP	WIDOW

Huck Finn

COFFIN	THATCHER	SARAH	LOFTUS	MOSES
HARNEY	SNAKE	CLEMENS	RAFT	SILAS
MISSISSIPPI	HANNIBAL	FREE SPACE	CIVILIZED	BUCK
HARKNESS	MISSOURI	BOGGS	OATH	RIVERBOATS
FISHING	FREEDOM	HOG	WIDOW	PAP

Huck Finn

PAP	GRANGERFORDS	TOM	RIVERBOATS	FREEDOM
SALLY	FISHING	WHISKEY	MATTRESS	TWAIN
WATSON	WALTER	FREE SPACE	SILAS	CABIN
NATURE	MOSES	OATH	CLEMENS	SARAH
HUCK	WIDOW	LUCK	COFFIN	EDUCATION

Huck Finn

RELIGION	GANG	JIM	RAFT	ISLAND
WILKS	SNAKE	HAIRBALL	HANNIBAL	HARKNESS
CIVILIZED	HARNEY	FREE SPACE	MISSISSIPPI	MISSOURI
KING	BUCK	TURNER	SLAVE	BOGGS
LOFTUS	HOG	ESCAPE	EDUCATION	COFFIN

Huck Finn

POLLY	NATURE	MATTRESS	COFFIN	FREEDOM
GRANGERFORDS	OATH	SLAVE	LUCK	LOFTUS
FISHING	WHISKEY	FREE SPACE	SNAKE	GANG
TURNER	SALLY	HAIRBALL	CABIN	WILKS
MISSISSIPPI	EDUCATION	SARAH	HANNIBAL	MISSOURI

Huck Finn

BUCK	JIM	MOSES	HARNEY	RIVERBOATS
ISLAND	THATCHER	WATSON	HUCK	RAFT
BOGGS	SILAS	FREE SPACE	PAP	KING
TOM	WIDOW	TWAIN	HARKNESS	HOG
WALTER	ESCAPE	CLEMENS	MISSOURI	HANNIBAL

Huck Finn

WHISKEY	SALLY	WATSON	TWAIN	FREEDOM
THATCHER	POLLY	PAP	RAFT	WALTER
SILAS	SARAH	FREE SPACE	TURNER	EDUCATION
HANNIBAL	HOG	CABIN	RIVERBOATS	LOFTUS
GANG	OATH	BUCK	TOM	MISSISSIPPI

Huck Finn

HARNEY	LUCK	JIM	BOGGS	CLEMENS
MATTRESS	KING	HUCK	COFFIN	SNAKE
NATURE	RELIGION	FREE SPACE	HARKNESS	ISLAND
WIDOW	HAIRBALL	CIVILIZED	WILKS	FISHING
GRANGERFORDS	MISSOURI	ESCAPE	MISSISSIPPI	TOM

Huck Finn

NATURE	LUCK	HARKNESS	CIVILIZED	MISSISSIPPI
GRANGERFORDS	RAFT	MATTRESS	FREEDOM	CABIN
SNAKE	SARAH	FREE SPACE	OATH	RELIGION
HUCK	TWAIN	KING	SLAVE	SILAS
LOFTUS	HARNEY	WALTER	TOM	HOG

Huck Finn

HANNIBAL	MOSES	BUCK	WATSON	PAP
THATCHER	EDUCATION	GANG	WILKS	ISLAND
POLLY	BOGGS	FREE SPACE	SALLY	CLEMENS
COFFIN	JIM	TURNER	WIDOW	FISHING
MISSOURI	RIVERBOATS	ESCAPE	HOG	TOM

Huck Finn

TURNER	HAIRBALL	CABIN	SALLY	PAP
LOFTUS	RELIGION	MISSISSIPPI	WHISKEY	SARAH
BOGGS	CLEMENS	FREE SPACE	WALTER	KING
CIVILIZED	WATSON	HANNIBAL	GANG	GRANGERFORDS
COFFIN	THATCHER	MATTRESS	ESCAPE	WIDOW

Huck Finn

OATH	LUCK	MOSES	SILAS	RAFT
HUCK	TOM	EDUCATION	MISSOURI	SNAKE
WILKS	FREEDOM	FREE SPACE	FISHING	ISLAND
RIVERBOATS	HARNEY	NATURE	JIM	POLLY
TWAIN	HARKNESS	HOG	WIDOW	ESCAPE

Huck Finn

SNAKE	LUCK	EDUCATION	TWAIN	CLEMENS
WALTER	RAFT	SLAVE	GRANGERFORDS	SILAS
MOSES	MISSOURI	FREE SPACE	JIM	FREEDOM
SARAH	MISSISSIPPI	OATH	HAIRBALL	BOGGS
BUCK	HANNIBAL	WATSON	POLLY	TURNER

Huck Finn

GANG	MATTRESS	RIVERBOATS	TOM	FISHING
HARNEY	SALLY	WHISKEY	THATCHER	ISLAND
NATURE	PAP	FREE SPACE	WILKS	CIVILIZED
COFFIN	HUCK	RELIGION	WIDOW	CABIN
HOG	ESCAPE	KING	TURNER	POLLY

Huck Finn

ISLAND	TURNER	RIVERBOATS	SALLY	NATURE
HAIRBALL	KING	HUCK	PAP	SLAVE
GANG	JIM	FREE SPACE	GRANGERFORDS	HARKNESS
HOG	MISSISSIPPI	POLLY	SNAKE	SARAH
SILAS	CIVILIZED	HANNIBAL	THATCHER	MOSES

Huck Finn

LUCK	FISHING	FREEDOM	HARNEY	WIDOW
RELIGION	BUCK	WILKS	BOGGS	OATH
EDUCATION	RAFT	FREE SPACE	WHISKEY	WALTER
CLEMENS	ESCAPE	MATTRESS	LOFTUS	CABIN
MISSOURI	WATSON	TOM	MOSES	THATCHER

Huck Finn

RIVERBOATS	SALLY	FREEDOM	SNAKE	PAP
TOM	MOSES	ESCAPE	HAIRBALL	HOG
HUCK	GRANGERFORDS	FREE SPACE	KING	OATH
POLLY	HANNIBAL	LOFTUS	WILKS	HARKNESS
SLAVE	EDUCATION	LUCK	JIM	SILAS

Huck Finn

HARNEY	ISLAND	CABIN	MATTRESS	COFFIN
GANG	BUCK	MISSISSIPPI	BOGGS	TURNER
RELIGION	CLEMENS	FREE SPACE	WHISKEY	WIDOW
TWAIN	MISSOURI	WATSON	FISHING	SARAH
NATURE	RAFT	THATCHER	SILAS	JIM

Huck Finn Vocabulary Word List

No.	Word	Clue/Definition
1.	ABOLITIONIST	Person against slavery
2.	ABREAST	Side by side
3.	ADDLED	Confused
4.	ADMIRABLE	Deserving admiration
5.	AFFLICTED	Handicapped
6.	AMPUTATE	Cut off
7.	BERTH	Place to sleep
8.	BRASH	Uninhibited; tactless; impudent
9.	BRISKEN	Make more lively; brighten
10.	BYGONES	Past happenings
11.	CANDID	Characterized by openness; straightforward
12.	CAVORTING	Extravagant behavior
13.	COAXING	Obtaining by persistent persuasion
14.	COLLAR	Seize or detain; grab and hold
15.	COMMENCED	Began
16.	CONFOUND	Cause to become confused or perplexed
17.	CONVENIENCES	Things that increase comfort or save work
18.	COUNTERFEIT	Fake; not real
19.	DERRICK	A crane
20.	DISMAL	Gloomy
21.	DISPOSITION	Inclination; attitude
22.	DISTINCTIONS	Differences
23.	DISTRACTED	Pulled in conflicting emotional directions
24.	DOXOLOJER	Kind of hymn
25.	ENCHANTMENT	Magic; sorcery
26.	ENCORES	Calls for repeat performances
27.	EVADE	Escape or avoid by cleverness or deceit
28.	FACULTIES	Any of the powers possessed by the human mind
29.	FAGGED	Exhausted
30.	FEUD	A hereditary fight
31.	FROCK	Woman's dress
32.	HAIL	Call to
33.	HUFFY	Fit of anger or annoyance
34.	IMPUDENT	Characterized by offensive boldness
35.	INSURRECTION	Act or instance of open revolt
36.	LAMENTED	Grieved
37.	LANGUISH	Faint; feeble; sickly
38.	LATH	Building materials
39.	LOLLED	Relaxed
40.	MELODEUM	Small reed organ
41.	MESMERISM	Hypnotism
42.	MORTIFICATION	Humiliation; embarrassment
43.	MOURNFUL	Sad
44.	OBSEQUIES	Funeral rites
45.	PALAVERING	Making idle talk
46.	PALLET	Temporary bed made from bedding arranged on the floor
47.	PASSEL	Bunch
48.	PENSIVE	Thoughtful
49.	PETRIFIED	Turned to stone
50.	PHRENOLOGY	Reading a person's future by examining their skull
51.	PIOUS	Religious; reverent

Huck Finn Vocabulary Word List Continued

No.	Word	Clue/Definition
52.	PREJUDICED	Having a preconceived preference
53.	QUICKSILVER	Mercury
54.	RANSACKED	Searched thoroughly but hastily
55.	RANSOMED	Freed from captivity for a price
56.	RASPY	Grating; harsh
57.	RUMMAGING	Rooting through as if searching
58.	SANCTIFIED	Holy
59.	SHROUD	Cloth used to wrap a body for burial
60.	SOLEMN	Having a respectful calm
61.	SOLILOQUY	Dramatic monologue
62.	SPECULATE	Make a risky financial transaction
63.	STANCHION	Post of timber or iron for support
64.	STAVING	Putting off; delaying
65.	STEALTHY	Acting with quiet caution
66.	SUBLIME	Excellent; having a sense of grandeur
67.	SULTRY	Very humid and hot
68.	TEDIOUS	Tiresome by reason of length; boring
69.	TEMPERANCE	Moderation; sobriety
70.	UNFURLED	Spread out
71.	VICTUALS	Food
72.	WADDING	Material for stopping charge in a gun
73.	WARBLING	Singing
74.	WAYLAY	Lie in wait for and attack as in an ambush
75.	YAWL	Small boat

Copyrighted

Huck Finn Vocabulary Fill In The Blanks 1

_____ 1. Mercury

_____ 2. Any of the powers possessed by the human mind

_____ 3. Kind of hymn

_____ 4. Food

_____ 5. Small boat

_____ 6. Singing

_____ 7. Turned to stone

_____ 8. Characterized by openness; straightforward

_____ 9. Gloomy

_____ 10. Uninhibited; tactless; impudent

_____ 11. Spread out

_____ 12. Deserving admiration

_____ 13. Things that increase comfort or save work

_____ 14. Dramatic monologue

_____ 15. Magic; sorcery

_____ 16. Calls for repeat performances

_____ 17. Small reed organ

_____ 18. Grieved

_____ 19. Humiliation; embarrassment

_____ 20. Material for stopping charge in a gun

Huck Finn Vocabulary Fill In The Blanks 1 Answer Key

QUICKSILVER	1.	Mercury
FACULTIES	2.	Any of the powers possessed by the human mind
DOXOLOJER	3.	Kind of hymn
VICTUALS	4.	Food
YAWL	5.	Small boat
WARBLING	6.	Singing
PETRIFIED	7.	Turned to stone
CANDID	8.	Characterized by openness; straightforward
DISMAL	9.	Gloomy
BRASH	10.	Uninhibited; tactless; impudent
UNFURLED	11.	Spread out
ADMIRABLE	12.	Deserving admiration
CONVENIENCES	13.	Things that increase comfort or save work
SOLILOQUY	14.	Dramatic monologue
ENCHANTMENT	15.	Magic; sorcery
ENCORES	16.	Calls for repeat performances
MELODEUM	17.	Small reed organ
LAMENTED	18.	Grieved
MORTIFICATION	19.	Humiliation; embarrassment
WADDING	20.	Material for stopping charge in a gun

Huck Finn Vocabulary Fill In The Blanks 2

_____
_____
_____
_____
_____
_____
_____
_____
_____
_____
_____
_____
_____
_____
_____
_____
_____
_____
_____
_____

1. Characterized by openness; straightforward
2. Searched thoroughly but hastily
3. Obtaining by persistent persuasion
4. Characterized by offensive boldness
5. Religious; reverent
6. Gloomy
7. Act or instance of open revolt
8. Food
9. Uninhibited; tactless; impudent
10. Escape or avoid by cleverness or deceit
11. Magic; sorcery
12. A hereditary fight
13. Side by side
14. Thoughtful
15. Small boat
16. Dramatic monologue
17. Cut off
18. Faint; feeble; sickly
19. Person against slavery
20. Singing

Huck Finn Vocabulary Fill In The Blanks 2 Answer Key

CANDID	1. Characterized by openness; straightforward
RANSACKED	2. Searched thoroughly but hastily
COAXING	3. Obtaining by persistent persuasion
IMPUDENT	4. Characterized by offensive boldness
PIOUS	5. Religious; reverent
DISMAL	6. Gloomy
INSURRECTION	7. Act or instance of open revolt
VICTUALS	8. Food
BRASH	9. Uninhibited; tactless; impudent
EVADE	10. Escape or avoid by cleverness or deceit
ENCHANTMENT	11. Magic; sorcery
FEUD	12. A hereditary fight
ABREAST	13. Side by side
PENSIVE	14. Thoughtful
YAWL	15. Small boat
SOLILOQUY	16. Dramatic monologue
AMPUTATE	17. Cut off
LANGUISH	18. Faint; feeble; sickly
ABOLITIONIST	19. Person against slavery
WARBLING	20. Singing

Huck Finn Vocabulary Fill In The Blanks 3

_____ 1. Gloomy

_____ 2. Make a risky financial transaction

_____ 3. Magic; sorcery

_____ 4. Uninhibited; tactless; impudent

_____ 5. Material for stopping charge in a gun

_____ 6. Extravagant behavior

_____ 7. Thoughtful

_____ 8. Cut off

_____ 9. Escape or avoid by cleverness or deceit

_____ 10. Differences

_____ 11. Act or instance of open revolt

_____ 12. Call to

_____ 13. Small boat

_____ 14. Tiresome by reason of length; boring

_____ 15. Mercury

_____ 16. Make more lively; brighten

_____ 17. Lie in wait for and attack as in an ambush

_____ 18. Funeral rites

_____ 19. Seize or detain; grab and hold

_____ 20. Place to sleep

Huck Finn Vocabulary Fill In The Blanks 3 Answer Key

DISMAL	1.	Gloomy
SPECULATE	2.	Make a risky financial transaction
ENCHANTMENT	3.	Magic; sorcery
BRASH	4.	Uninhibited; tactless; impudent
WADDING	5.	Material for stopping charge in a gun
CAVORTING	6.	Extravagant behavior
PENSIVE	7.	Thoughtful
AMPUTATE	8.	Cut off
EVADE	9.	Escape or avoid by cleverness or deceit
DISTINCTIONS	10.	Differences
INSURRECTION	11.	Act or instance of open revolt
HAIL	12.	Call to
YAWL	13.	Small boat
TEDIOUS	14.	Tiresome by reason of length; boring
QUICKSILVER	15.	Mercury
BRISKEN	16.	Make more lively; brighten
WAYLAY	17.	Lie in wait for and attack as in an ambush
OBSEQUIES	18.	Funeral rites
COLLAR	19.	Seize or detain; grab and hold
BERTH	20.	Place to sleep

Huck Finn Vocabulary Fill In The Blanks 4

_____ 1. Confused
_____ 2. Reading a person's future by examining their skull
_____ 3. Gloomy
_____ 4. Lie in wait for and attack as in an ambush
_____ 5. Characterized by offensive boldness
_____ 6. Spread out
_____ 7. Bunch
_____ 8. Person against slavery
_____ 9. Holy
_____ 10. Hypnotism
_____ 11. Excellent; having a sense of grandeur
_____ 12. Fake; not real
_____ 13. Characterized by openness; straightforward
_____ 14. Food
_____ 15. Deserving admiration
_____ 16. Mercury
_____ 17. Rooting through as if searching
_____ 18. Thoughtful
_____ 19. Having a respectful calm
_____ 20. Handicapped

Huck Finn Vocabulary Fill In The Blanks 4 Answer Key

ADDLED	1.	Confused
PHRENOLOGY	2.	Reading a person's future by examining their skull
DISMAL	3.	Gloomy
WAYLAY	4.	Lie in wait for and attack as in an ambush
IMPUDENT	5.	Characterized by offensive boldness
UNFURLED	6.	Spread out
PASSEL	7.	Bunch
ABOLITIONIST	8.	Person against slavery
SANCTIFIED	9.	Holy
MESMERISM	10.	Hypnotism
SUBLIME	11.	Excellent; having a sense of grandeur
COUNTERFEIT	12.	Fake; not real
CANDID	13.	Characterized by openness; straightforward
VICTUALS	14.	Food
ADMIRABLE	15.	Deserving admiration
QUICKSILVER	16.	Mercury
RUMMAGING	17.	Rooting through as if searching
PENSIVE	18.	Thoughtful
SOLEMN	19.	Having a respectful calm
AFFLICTED	20.	Handicapped

Huck Finn Vocabulary Matching 1

___ 1. COAXING   A. Having a preconceived preference
___ 2. WADDING   B. Mercury
___ 3. CONVENIENCES   C. Handicapped
___ 4. ADMIRABLE   D. Things that increase comfort or save work
___ 5. CANDID   E. Seize or detain; grab and hold
___ 6. SUBLIME   F. Food
___ 7. SHROUD   G. Inclination; attitude
___ 8. EVADE   H. Lie in wait for and attack as in an ambush
___ 9. QUICKSILVER   I. Faint; feeble; sickly
___10. AFFLICTED   J. Deserving admiration
___11. PASSEL   K. Bunch
___12. VICTUALS   L. Obtaining by persistent persuasion
___13. LANGUISH   M. Funeral rites
___14. ENCHANTMENT   N. Acting with quiet caution
___15. TEMPERANCE   O. Began
___16. RASPY   P. Side by side
___17. FEUD   Q. A hereditary fight
___18. OBSEQUIES   R. Grating; harsh
___19. COLLAR   S. Excellent; having a sense of grandeur
___20. PREJUDICED   T. Characterized by openness; straightforward
___21. ABREAST   U. Cloth used to wrap a body for burial
___22. WAYLAY   V. Material for stopping charge in a gun
___23. DISPOSITION   W. Escape or avoid by cleverness or deceit
___24. COMMENCED   X. Magic; sorcery
___25. STEALTHY   Y. Moderation; sobriety

Huck Finn Vocabulary Matching 1 Answer Key

L - 1. COAXING	A. Having a preconceived preference
V - 2. WADDING	B. Mercury
D - 3. CONVENIENCES	C. Handicapped
J - 4. ADMIRABLE	D. Things that increase comfort or save work
T - 5. CANDID	E. Seize or detain; grab and hold
S - 6. SUBLIME	F. Food
U - 7. SHROUD	G. Inclination; attitude
W - 8. EVADE	H. Lie in wait for and attack as in an ambush
B - 9. QUICKSILVER	I. Faint; feeble; sickly
C -10. AFFLICTED	J. Deserving admiration
K -11. PASSEL	K. Bunch
F -12. VICTUALS	L. Obtaining by persistent persuasion
I -13. LANGUISH	M. Funeral rites
X -14. ENCHANTMENT	N. Acting with quiet caution
Y -15. TEMPERANCE	O. Began
R -16. RASPY	P. Side by side
Q -17. FEUD	Q. A hereditary fight
M -18. OBSEQUIES	R. Grating; harsh
E -19. COLLAR	S. Excellent; having a sense of grandeur
A -20. PREJUDICED	T. Characterized by openness; straightforward
P -21. ABREAST	U. Cloth used to wrap a body for burial
H -22. WAYLAY	V. Material for stopping charge in a gun
G -23. DISPOSITION	W. Escape or avoid by cleverness or deceit
O -24. COMMENCED	X. Magic; sorcery
N -25. STEALTHY	Y. Moderation; sobriety

Huck Finn Vocabulary Matching 2

___ 1. SULTRY A. Extravagant behavior
___ 2. WARBLING B. Lie in wait for and attack as in an ambush
___ 3. LATH C. Rooting through as if searching
___ 4. COUNTERFEIT D. Obtaining by persistent persuasion
___ 5. RUMMAGING E. Fake; not real
___ 6. SANCTIFIED F. Humiliation; embarrassment
___ 7. COMMENCED G. Hypnotism
___ 8. WAYLAY H. Very humid and hot
___ 9. SOLILOQUY I. Cloth used to wrap a body for burial
___ 10. STEALTHY J. Material for stopping charge in a gun
___ 11. MESMERISM K. Person against slavery
___ 12. SUBLIME L. Grieved
___ 13. COAXING M. Began
___ 14. PETRIFIED N. Inclination; attitude
___ 15. RANSACKED O. A crane
___ 16. WADDING P. Building materials
___ 17. SHROUD Q. Searched thoroughly but hastily
___ 18. ABOLITIONIST R. Dramatic monologue
___ 19. YAWL S. Singing
___ 20. DISPOSITION T. Excellent; having a sense of grandeur
___ 21. LAMENTED U. Acting with quiet caution
___ 22. MORTIFICATION V. Turned to stone
___ 23. CAVORTING W. Small boat
___ 24. DISMAL X. Holy
___ 25. DERRICK Y. Gloomy

Huck Finn Vocabulary Matching 2 Answer Key

H - 1. SULTRY	A.	Extravagant behavior
S - 2. WARBLING	B.	Lie in wait for and attack as in an ambush
P - 3. LATH	C.	Rooting through as if searching
E - 4. COUNTERFEIT	D.	Obtaining by persistent persuasion
C - 5. RUMMAGING	E.	Fake; not real
X - 6. SANCTIFIED	F.	Humiliation; embarrassment
M - 7. COMMENCED	G.	Hypnotism
B - 8. WAYLAY	H.	Very humid and hot
R - 9. SOLILOQUY	I.	Cloth used to wrap a body for burial
U - 10. STEALTHY	J.	Material for stopping charge in a gun
G - 11. MESMERISM	K.	Person against slavery
T - 12. SUBLIME	L.	Grieved
D - 13. COAXING	M.	Began
V - 14. PETRIFIED	N.	Inclination; attitude
Q - 15. RANSACKED	O.	A crane
J - 16. WADDING	P.	Building materials
I - 17. SHROUD	Q.	Searched thoroughly but hastily
K - 18. ABOLITIONIST	R.	Dramatic monologue
W - 19. YAWL	S.	Singing
N - 20. DISPOSITION	T.	Excellent; having a sense of grandeur
L - 21. LAMENTED	U.	Acting with quiet caution
F - 22. MORTIFICATION	V.	Turned to stone
A - 23. CAVORTING	W.	Small boat
Y - 24. DISMAL	X.	Holy
O - 25. DERRICK	Y.	Gloomy

Huck Finn Vocabulary Matching 3

___ 1. CONFOUND   A. Calls for repeat performances
___ 2. DISPOSITION   B. Began
___ 3. SHROUD   C. Inclination; attitude
___ 4. PASSEL   D. Kind of hymn
___ 5. LAMENTED   E. Extravagant behavior
___ 6. PETRIFIED   F. Material for stopping charge in a gun
___ 7. DISMAL   G. Funeral rites
___ 8. ABREAST   H. Make more lively; brighten
___ 9. OBSEQUIES   I. Seize or detain; grab and hold
___ 10. DOXOLOJER   J. Grating; harsh
___ 11. RASPY   K. Side by side
___ 12. DISTINCTIONS   L. Things that increase comfort or save work
___ 13. MELODEUM   M. Confused
___ 14. ABOLITIONIST   N. Person against slavery
___ 15. CONVENIENCES   O. Cause to become confused or perplexed
___ 16. WADDING   P. Pulled in conflicting emotional directions
___ 17. DISTRACTED   Q. Post of timber or iron for support
___ 18. COMMENCED   R. Grieved
___ 19. COLLAR   S. Cloth used to wrap a body for burial
___ 20. CAVORTING   T. Gloomy
___ 21. BRISKEN   U. Bunch
___ 22. ADDLED   V. Sad
___ 23. MOURNFUL   W. Turned to stone
___ 24. ENCORES   X. Differences
___ 25. STANCHION   Y. Small reed organ

Huck Finn Vocabulary Matching 3 Answer Key

O - 1. CONFOUND		A. Calls for repeat performances
C - 2. DISPOSITION		B. Began
S - 3. SHROUD		C. Inclination; attitude
U - 4. PASSEL		D. Kind of hymn
R - 5. LAMENTED		E. Extravagant behavior
W - 6. PETRIFIED		F. Material for stopping charge in a gun
T - 7. DISMAL		G. Funeral rites
K - 8. ABREAST		H. Make more lively; brighten
G - 9. OBSEQUIES		I. Seize or detain; grab and hold
D - 10. DOXOLOJER		J. Grating; harsh
J - 11. RASPY		K. Side by side
X - 12. DISTINCTIONS		L. Things that increase comfort or save work
Y - 13. MELODEUM		M. Confused
N - 14. ABOLITIONIST		N. Person against slavery
L - 15. CONVENIENCES		O. Cause to become confused or perplexed
F - 16. WADDING		P. Pulled in conflicting emotional directions
P - 17. DISTRACTED		Q. Post of timber or iron for support
B - 18. COMMENCED		R. Grieved
I - 19. COLLAR		S. Cloth used to wrap a body for burial
E - 20. CAVORTING		T. Gloomy
H - 21. BRISKEN		U. Bunch
M - 22. ADDLED		V. Sad
V - 23. MOURNFUL		W. Turned to stone
A - 24. ENCORES		X. Differences
Q - 25. STANCHION		Y. Small reed organ

Huck Finn Vocabulary Matching 4

___ 1. INSURRECTION   A. Make more lively; brighten

___ 2. ENCORES   B. Act or instance of open revolt

___ 3. PALAVERING   C. Extravagant behavior

___ 4. CONFOUND   D. Obtaining by persistent persuasion

___ 5. SHROUD   E. Small reed organ

___ 6. QUICKSILVER   F. Began

___ 7. CAVORTING   G. Seize or detain; grab and hold

___ 8. DISPOSITION   H. Relaxed

___ 9. LOLLED   I. Inclination; attitude

___ 10. PREJUDICED   J. Mercury

___ 11. FROCK   K. Reading a person's future by examining their skull

___ 12. ENCHANTMENT   L. Having a preconceived preference

___ 13. HAIL   M. Making idle talk

___ 14. BRISKEN   N. Magic; sorcery

___ 15. COAXING   O. Call to

___ 16. PALLET   P. Faint; feeble; sickly

___ 17. PETRIFIED   Q. Woman's dress

___ 18. COMMENCED   R. Temporary bed made from bedding arranged on the floor

___ 19. RANSOMED   S. Rooting through as if searching

___ 20. PHRENOLOGY   T. Calls for repeat performances

___ 21. RUMMAGING   U. Putting off; delaying

___ 22. MELODEUM   V. Freed from captivity for a price

___ 23. STAVING   W. Turned to stone

___ 24. LANGUISH   X. Cloth used to wrap a body for burial

___ 25. COLLAR   Y. Cause to become confused or perplexed

Huck Finn Vocabulary Matching 4 Answer Key

B - 1. INSURRECTION	A.	Make more lively; brighten
T - 2. ENCORES	B.	Act or instance of open revolt
M - 3. PALAVERING	C.	Extravagant behavior
Y - 4. CONFOUND	D.	Obtaining by persistent persuasion
X - 5. SHROUD	E.	Small reed organ
J - 6. QUICKSILVER	F.	Began
C - 7. CAVORTING	G.	Seize or detain; grab and hold
I - 8. DISPOSITION	H.	Relaxed
H - 9. LOLLED	I.	Inclination; attitude
L - 10. PREJUDICED	J.	Mercury
Q - 11. FROCK	K.	Reading a person's future by examining their skull
N - 12. ENCHANTMENT	L.	Having a preconceived preference
O - 13. HAIL	M.	Making idle talk
A - 14. BRISKEN	N.	Magic; sorcery
D - 15. COAXING	O.	Call to
R - 16. PALLET	P.	Faint; feeble; sickly
W - 17. PETRIFIED	Q.	Woman's dress
F - 18. COMMENCED	R.	Temporary bed made from bedding arranged on the floor
V - 19. RANSOMED	S.	Rooting through as if searching
K - 20. PHRENOLOGY	T.	Calls for repeat performances
S - 21. RUMMAGING	U.	Putting off; delaying
E - 22. MELODEUM	V.	Freed from captivity for a price
U - 23. STAVING	W.	Turned to stone
P - 24. LANGUISH	X.	Cloth used to wrap a body for burial
G - 25. COLLAR	Y.	Cause to become confused or perplexed

Huck Finn Vocabulary Magic Squares 1

Match the definition with the vocabulary word. Put your answers in the magic squares below. When your answers are correct, all columns and rows will add to the same number.

A. VICTUALS
B. CANDID
C. PREJUDICED
D. PETRIFIED
E. UNFURLED
F. WARBLING
G. PHRENOLOGY
H. COMMENCED
I. CONVENIENCES
J. WAYLAY
K. DERRICK
L. BYGONES
M. AMPUTATE
N. FROCK
O. PENSIVE
P. MOURNFUL

1. Began
2. Cut off
3. Characterized by openness; straightforward
4. A crane
5. Lie in wait for and attack as in an ambush
6. Having a preconceived preference
7. Sad
8. Spread out
9. Thoughtful
10. Singing
11. Things that increase comfort or save work
12. Turned to stone
13. Food
14. Past happenings
15. Reading a person's future by examining their skull
16. Woman's dress

A=	B=	C=	D=
E=	F=	G=	H=
I=	J=	K=	L=
M=	N=	O=	P=

Huck Finn Vocabulary Magic Squares 1 Answer Key

Match the definition with the vocabulary word. Put your answers in the magic squares below. When your answers are correct, all columns and rows will add to the same number.

A. VICTUALS
B. CANDID
C. PREJUDICED
D. PETRIFIED
E. UNFURLED
F. WARBLING
G. PHRENOLOGY
H. COMMENCED
I. CONVENIENCES
J. WAYLAY
K. DERRICK
L. BYGONES
M. AMPUTATE
N. FROCK
O. PENSIVE
P. MOURNFUL

1. Began
2. Cut off
3. Characterized by openness; straightforward
4. A crane
5. Lie in wait for and attack as in an ambush
6. Having a preconceived preference
7. Sad
8. Spread out
9. Thoughtful
10. Singing
11. Things that increase comfort or save work
12. Turned to stone
13. Food
14. Past happenings
15. Reading a person's future by examining their skull
16. Woman's dress

A=13	B=3	C=6	D=12
E=8	F=10	G=15	H=1
I=11	J=5	K=4	L=14
M=2	N=16	O=9	P=7

Huck Finn Vocabulary Magic Squares 2

Match the definition with the vocabulary word. Put your answers in the magic squares below. When your answers are correct, all columns and rows will add to the same number.

A. STEALTHY
B. CANDID
C. LANGUISH
D. SOLEMN
E. OBSEQUIES
F. BYGONES
G. WARBLING
H. PALLET
I. ABREAST
J. IMPUDENT
K. FAGGED
L. WAYLAY
M. FEUD
N. COLLAR
O. CAVORTING
P. DISTRACTED

1. Extravagant behavior
2. Characterized by offensive boldness
3. Temporary bed made from bedding arranged on the floor
4. Acting with quiet caution
5. Having a respectful calm
6. Funeral rites
7. Exhausted
8. Seize or detain; grab and hold
9. Past happenings
10. Faint; feeble; sickly
11. A hereditary fight
12. Lie in wait for and attack as in an ambush
13. Side by side
14. Pulled in conflicting emotional directions
15. Characterized by openness; straightforward
16. Singing

A=	B=	C=	D=
E=	F=	G=	H=
I=	J=	K=	L=
M=	N=	O=	P=

Huck Finn Vocabulary Magic Squares 2 Answer Key

Match the definition with the vocabulary word. Put your answers in the magic squares below. When your answers are correct, all columns and rows will add to the same number.

A. STEALTHY
B. CANDID
C. LANGUISH
D. SOLEMN
E. OBSEQUIES
F. BYGONES
G. WARBLING
H. PALLET
I. ABREAST
J. IMPUDENT
K. FAGGED
L. WAYLAY
M. FEUD
N. COLLAR
O. CAVORTING
P. DISTRACTED

1. Extravagant behavior
2. Characterized by offensive boldness
3. Temporary bed made from bedding arranged on the floor
4. Acting with quiet caution
5. Having a respectful calm
6. Funeral rites
7. Exhausted
8. Seize or detain; grab and hold
9. Past happenings
10. Faint; feeble; sickly
11. A hereditary fight
12. Lie in wait for and attack as in an ambush
13. Side by side
14. Pulled in conflicting emotional directions
15. Characterized by openness; straightforward
16. Singing

A=4	B=15	C=10	D=5
E=6	F=9	G=16	H=3
I=13	J=2	K=7	L=12
M=11	N=8	O=1	P=14

Huck Finn Vocabulary Magic Squares 3

Match the definition with the vocabulary word. Put your answers in the magic squares below. When your answers are correct, all columns and rows will add to the same number.

A. WADDING
B. DOXOLOJER
C. ADDLED
D. LAMENTED
E. SOLILOQUY
F. BRISKEN
G. YAWL
H. FROCK
I. SUBLIME
J. RANSOMED
K. SOLEMN
L. COLLAR
M. SULTRY
N. PALAVERING
O. VICTUALS
P. BRASH

1. Woman's dress
2. Material for stopping charge in a gun
3. Kind of hymn
4. Small boat
5. Freed from captivity for a price
6. Food
7. Uninhibited; tactless; impudent
8. Excellent; having a sense of grandeur
9. Having a respectful calm
10. Making idle talk
11. Very humid and hot
12. Seize or detain; grab and hold
13. Dramatic monologue
14. Grieved
15. Confused
16. Make more lively; brighten

A=	B=	C=	D=
E=	F=	G=	H=
I=	J=	K=	L=
M=	N=	O=	P=

Huck Finn Vocabulary Magic Squares 3 Answer Key

Match the definition with the vocabulary word. Put your answers in the magic squares below. When your answers are correct, all columns and rows will add to the same number.

A. WADDING
B. DOXOLOJER
C. ADDLED
D. LAMENTED
E. SOLILOQUY
F. BRISKEN
G. YAWL
H. FROCK
I. SUBLIME
J. RANSOMED
K. SOLEMN
L. COLLAR
M. SULTRY
N. PALAVERING
O. VICTUALS
P. BRASH

1. Woman's dress
2. Material for stopping charge in a gun
3. Kind of hymn
4. Small boat
5. Freed from captivity for a price
6. Food
7. Uninhibited; tactless; impudent
8. Excellent; having a sense of grandeur
9. Having a respectful calm
10. Making idle talk
11. Very humid and hot
12. Seize or detain; grab and hold
13. Dramatic monologue
14. Grieved
15. Confused
16. Make more lively; brighten

A=2	B=3	C=15	D=14
E=13	F=16	G=4	H=1
I=8	J=5	K=9	L=12
M=11	N=10	O=6	P=7

Huck Finn Vocabulary Magic Squares 4

Match the definition with the vocabulary word. Put your answers in the magic squares below. When your answers are correct, all columns and rows will add to the same number.

A. PASSEL
B. DISTRACTED
C. RANSOMED
D. YAWL
E. VICTUALS
F. EVADE
G. COUNTERFEIT
H. QUICKSILVER
I. BYGONES
J. CANDID
K. STEALTHY
L. DERRICK
M. IMPUDENT
N. PREJUDICED
O. FEUD
P. WAYLAY

1. Freed from captivity for a price
2. Characterized by openness; straightforward
3. Escape or avoid by cleverness or deceit
4. A hereditary fight
5. Lie in wait for and attack as in an ambush
6. Food
7. Past happenings
8. Small boat
9. Characterized by offensive boldness
10. Mercury
11. A crane
12. Bunch
13. Pulled in conflicting emotional directions
14. Acting with quiet caution
15. Fake; not real
16. Having a preconceived preference

A=	B=	C=	D=
E=	F=	G=	H=
I=	J=	K=	L=
M=	N=	O=	P=

Huck Finn Vocabulary Magic Squares 4 Answer Key

Match the definition with the vocabulary word. Put your answers in the magic squares below. When your answers are correct, all columns and rows will add to the same number.

A. PASSEL
B. DISTRACTED
C. RANSOMED
D. YAWL
E. VICTUALS
F. EVADE
G. COUNTERFEIT
H. QUICKSILVER
I. BYGONES
J. CANDID
K. STEALTHY
L. DERRICK
M. IMPUDENT
N. PREJUDICED
O. FEUD
P. WAYLAY

1. Freed from captivity for a price
2. Characterized by openness; straightforward
3. Escape or avoid by cleverness or deceit
4. A hereditary fight
5. Lie in wait for and attack as in an ambush
6. Food
7. Past happenings
8. Small boat
9. Characterized by offensive boldness
10. Mercury
11. A crane
12. Bunch
13. Pulled in conflicting emotional directions
14. Acting with quiet caution
15. Fake; not real
16. Having a preconceived preference

A=12	B=13	C=1	D=8
E=6	F=3	G=15	H=10
I=7	J=2	K=14	L=11
M=9	N=16	O=4	P=5

Huck Finn Vocabulary Word Search 1

Words are placed backwards, forward, diagonally, up and down. Clues listed below can help you find the words. Circle the hidden vocabulary words in the maze.

```
P S U N F U R L E D L A S D N D B T E Q
E A U G N I D D A W T A F W M Y E I V N
T W L B F X X F I W X C T F E H R E I N
R A T L L J J A G S D D D H L V T F S P
I Y W J E I W G K S T X I E O I H R N R
F L L F F T M G K E Y I D S S B C E E D
I A B R I S K E N C H A N T M E N T P C
E Y O X U N N D O N V Y W C S A A N E J
D C N L X C F N P E M H D L T L L U W D
K V T V O C F L A I W O N D U I X O D P
D R A R Z O Q A S N M S U C H D O C B W
Y E E B U M F N S E N E E R E U O N B S
U S R N R M Z G E V F P V L N A F V S V
Q V D R J E Y U L N S C L G X F S F F K
O B P C I N A I M O K O O I H T U Y Y Y
L Z I A G C V S W C L P N L A A D L Y D
I N O N X E K H T D M G V V L Q I P Y S
L G U D T D O B S E Q U I E S A S L W F
O F S I H D E K C A S N A R R A R T G F
S T E D I O U S K G G D U O R H S A R B
```

A crane (7)
A hereditary fight (4)
Began (9)
Building materials (4)
Bunch (6)
Call to (4)
Calls for repeat performances (7)
Cause to become confused or perplexed (8)
Characterized by openness; straightforward (6)
Cloth used to wrap a body for burial (6)
Differences (12)
Dramatic monologue (9)
Escape or avoid by cleverness or deceit (5)
Excellent; having a sense of grandeur (7)
Exhausted (6)
Faint; feeble; sickly (8)
Fake; not real (11)
Fit of anger or annoyance (5)
Funeral rites (9)
Gloomy (6)
Grating; harsh (5)
Handicapped (9)
Having a respectful calm (6)
Lie in wait for and attack as in an ambush (6)
Magic; sorcery (11)
Make a risky financial transaction (9)
Make more lively; brighten (7)
Material for stopping charge in a gun (7)
Obtaining by persistent persuasion (7)
Place to sleep (5)
Putting off; delaying (7)
Relaxed (6)
Religious; reverent (5)
Sad (8)
Searched thoroughly but hastily (9)
Seize or detain; grab and hold (6)
Side by side (7)
Small boat (4)
Spread out (8)
Temporary bed made from bedding arranged on the floor (6)
Things that increase comfort or save work (12)
Thoughtful (7)
Tiresome by reason of length; boring (7)
Turned to stone (9)
Uninhibited; tactless; impudent (5)
Very humid and hot (6)
Woman's dress (5)

Huck Finn Vocabulary Word Search 1 Answer Key

Words are placed backwards, forward, diagonally, up and down. Clues listed below can help you find the words. Circle the hidden vocabulary words in the maze.

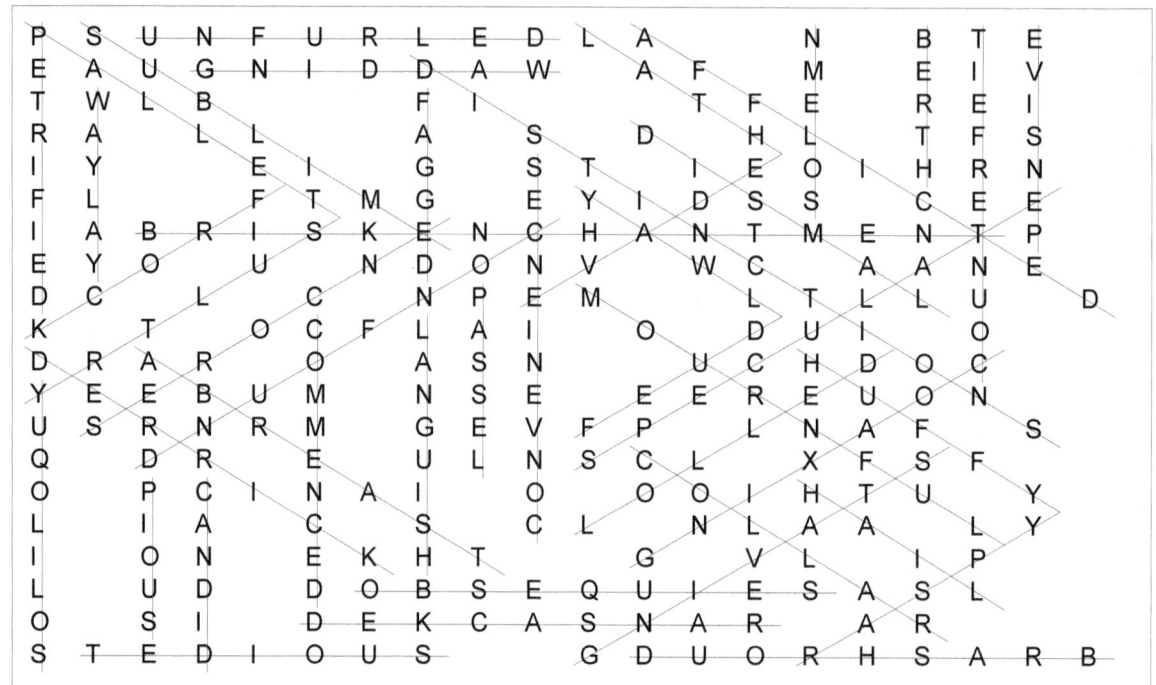

A crane (7)
A hereditary fight (4)
Began (9)
Building materials (4)
Bunch (6)
Call to (4)
Calls for repeat performances (7)
Cause to become confused or perplexed (8)
Characterized by openness; straightforward (6)
Cloth used to wrap a body for burial (6)
Differences (12)
Dramatic monologue (9)
Escape or avoid by cleverness or deceit (5)
Excellent; having a sense of grandeur (7)
Exhausted (6)
Faint; feeble; sickly (8)
Fake; not real (11)
Fit of anger or annoyance (5)
Funeral rites (9)
Gloomy (6)
Grating; harsh (5)
Handicapped (9)
Having a respectful calm (6)
Lie in wait for and attack as in an ambush (6)
Magic; sorcery (11)

Make a risky financial transaction (9)
Make more lively; brighten (7)
Material for stopping charge in a gun (7)
Obtaining by persistent persuasion (7)
Place to sleep (5)
Putting off; delaying (7)
Relaxed (6)
Religious; reverent (5)
Sad (8)
Searched thoroughly but hastily (9)
Seize or detain; grab and hold (6)
Side by side (7)
Small boat (4)
Spread out (8)
Temporary bed made from bedding arranged on the floor (6)
Things that increase comfort or save work (12)
Thoughtful (7)
Tiresome by reason of length; boring (7)
Turned to stone (9)
Uninhibited; tactless; impudent (5)
Very humid and hot (6)
Woman's dress (5)

Huck Finn Vocabulary Word Search 2

Words are placed backwards, forward, diagonally, up and down. Clues listed below can help you find the words. Circle the hidden vocabulary words in the maze.

```
E V A D E C N A R E P M E T P L X D F H
C Q K V M J H D R D P H S F V A E Y A H
M B C G Y H A F M E T J N H G C S R G P
C A V O R T I N G R E V I S N E P S G W
A O L D N R L S E R O C N E I A T D E Q
N P A W G F F B D I Q K M T L X Y U D L
D J H X N S O R T C R M D L B A R O B N
I Y Y B I L K U O K O Z E S R T T R R C
D L F Z V N O Y N C G T W O A L L H I L
P B T Q A Y G L P D K C A L W A U S S H
Y A W L T A D D L E D M B E G M S U K D
M P O B S E Q U I E S K R M N S O B E G
E M I L B U S P K D D B E N I I V P N E
L D M O G R P C S E G R A B D D I C T V
O B B W U A A V K M C A S E D Y C A V Q
D I S P O S I T I O N S T E A L T H Y P
E X F T N P B Q L S H H H L W U U F F W
U T L A M Y Z L C N D M Y X P Q A E F S
M S R S B B A Q R A S A R M T X L U U G
K L U F N R U O M R W P A P T P S D H C
```

A crane (7)
A hereditary fight (4)
Acting with quiet caution (8)
Began (9)
Building materials (4)
Bunch (6)
Call to (4)
Calls for repeat performances (7)
Cause to become confused or perplexed (8)
Characterized by openness; straightforward (6)
Cloth used to wrap a body for burial (6)
Confused (6)
Cut off (8)
Escape or avoid by cleverness or deceit (5)
Excellent; having a sense of grandeur (7)
Exhausted (6)
Extravagant behavior (9)
Fit of anger or annoyance (5)
Food (8)
Freed from captivity for a price (8)
Funeral rites (9)
Gloomy (6)
Grating; harsh (5)
Having a respectful calm (6)
Inclination; attitude (11)

Lie in wait for and attack as in an ambush (6)
Make more lively; brighten (7)
Material for stopping charge in a gun (7)
Moderation; sobriety (10)
Obtaining by persistent persuasion (7)
Place to sleep (5)
Putting off; delaying (7)
Relaxed (6)
Religious; reverent (5)
Sad (8)
Searched thoroughly but hastily (9)
Seize or detain; grab and hold (6)
Side by side (7)
Singing (8)
Small boat (4)
Small reed organ (8)
Temporary bed made from bedding arranged on the floor (6)
Thoughtful (7)
Tiresome by reason of length; boring (7)
Uninhibited; tactless; impudent (5)
Very humid and hot (6)
Woman's dress (5)

Huck Finn Vocabulary Word Search 2 Answer Key

Words are placed backwards, forward, diagonally, up and down. Clues listed below can help you find the words. Circle the hidden vocabulary words in the maze.

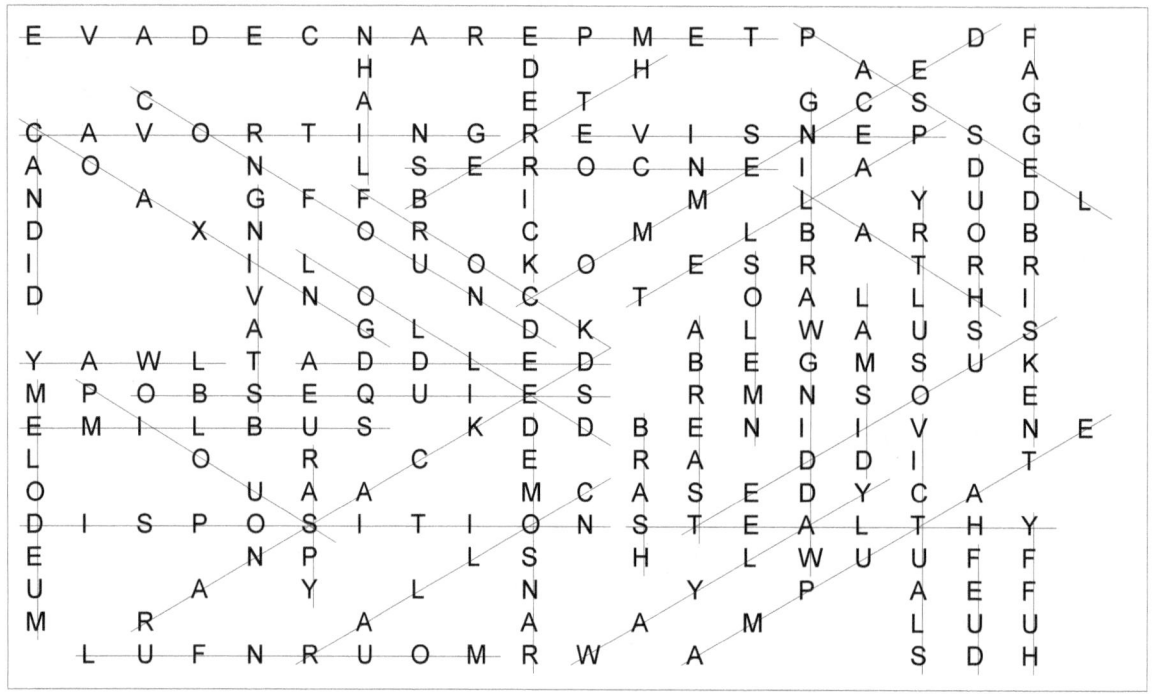

A crane (7)
A hereditary fight (4)
Acting with quiet caution (8)
Began (9)
Building materials (4)
Bunch (6)
Call to (4)
Calls for repeat performances (7)
Cause to become confused or perplexed (8)
Characterized by openness; straightforward (6)
Cloth used to wrap a body for burial (6)
Confused (6)
Cut off (8)
Escape or avoid by cleverness or deceit (5)
Excellent; having a sense of grandeur (7)
Exhausted (6)
Extravagant behavior (9)
Fit of anger or annoyance (5)
Food (8)
Freed from captivity for a price (8)
Funeral rites (9)
Gloomy (6)
Grating; harsh (5)
Having a respectful calm (6)
Inclination; attitude (11)

Lie in wait for and attack as in an ambush (6)
Make more lively; brighten (7)
Material for stopping charge in a gun (7)
Moderation; sobriety (10)
Obtaining by persistent persuasion (7)
Place to sleep (5)
Putting off; delaying (7)
Relaxed (6)
Religious; reverent (5)
Sad (8)
Searched thoroughly but hastily (9)
Seize or detain; grab and hold (6)
Side by side (7)
Singing (8)
Small boat (4)
Small reed organ (8)
Temporary bed made from bedding arranged on the floor (6)
Thoughtful (7)
Tiresome by reason of length; boring (7)
Uninhibited; tactless; impudent (5)
Very humid and hot (6)
Woman's dress (5)

Huck Finn Vocabulary Word Search 3

Words are placed backwards, forward, diagonally, up and down. Words listed below are included in the maze. Circle the hidden vocabulary words in the maze.

```
S H R O U D E M O S N A R M P A S S E L
U O N X I V C X F L S A E X F Y T P T P
O C L D Q K N F B J L L V F H T N G A P
I J N E W L A L X L O V L S N E O N T F
P A Z K M G R P O D B I I R O D I I U H
C W N N G N E C E G C U S C I I H R P R
S S A E L X P U N T G S K B T O C E M Y
A N D R B N M W E N I T C P I U N V A C
N O W W B K E D A D M A I L S S A A R K
C I E A R L T L E X P V U F O U T L P M
T T N Y D Q I T T P U I Q Y P L S A S Y
I C C L Z D C N Q E D N P G S T R P V N
F N O A F A I N G N E G P O I R S W V V
I I R Y R A K N P S N K C L D Y T D L Z
E T E T H D C T G I T H N O Q S W U W W
D S S M S D E U V V S S B N A M Y E A C
D I S M A L O L L E D A V E H U F F Y L
D D R L L E V K N T Y R R R G N P F J
B X K A A D Y O C G I B V H X T S Z H F
S H P M J T G X F T A E P P D A H L A V
F R O C K Y H S G N E K S I R B C P I D
E M I L B U S R U M M A G I N G F G L G
```

ABREAST	DISPOSITION	IMPUDENT	QUICKSILVER	TEDIOUS
ADDLED	DISTINCTIONS	LANGUISH	RANSOMED	TEMPERANCE
AFFLICTED	DISTRACTED	LATH	RASPY	VICTUALS
AMPUTATE	ENCORES	LOLLED	RUMMAGING	WADDING
BERTH	EVADE	MELODEUM	SANCTIFIED	WARBLING
BRASH	FACULTIES	PALAVERING	SHROUD	WAYLAY
BRISKEN	FAGGED	PALLET	SOLEMN	YAWL
BYGONES	FEUD	PASSEL	STANCHION	
CANDID	FROCK	PENSIVE	STAVING	
COLLAR	HAIL	PHRENOLOGY	SUBLIME	
DISMAL	HUFFY	PIOUS	SULTRY	

Huck Finn Vocabulary Word Search 3 Answer Key

Words are placed backwards, forward, diagonally, up and down. Words listed below are included in the maze. Circle the hidden vocabulary words in the maze.

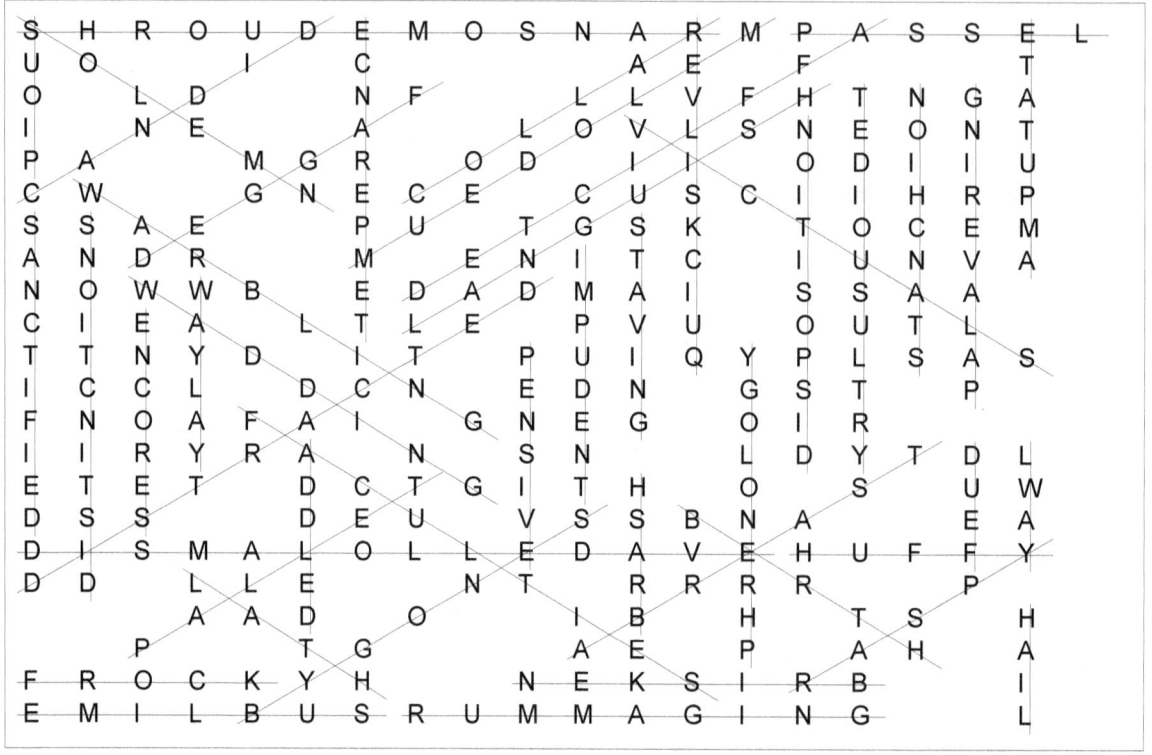

ABREAST	DISPOSITION	IMPUDENT	QUICKSILVER	TEDIOUS
ADDLED	DISTINCTIONS	LANGUISH	RANSOMED	TEMPERANCE
AFFLICTED	DISTRACTED	LATH	RASPY	VICTUALS
AMPUTATE	ENCORES	LOLLED	RUMMAGING	WADDING
BERTH	EVADE	MELODEUM	SANCTIFIED	WARBLING
BRASH	FACULTIES	PALAVERING	SHROUD	WAYLAY
BRISKEN	FAGGED	PALLET	SOLEMN	YAWL
BYGONES	FEUD	PASSEL	STANCHION	
CANDID	FROCK	PENSIVE	STAVING	
COLLAR	HAIL	PHRENOLOGY	SUBLIME	
DISMAL	HUFFY	PIOUS	SULTRY	

Huck Finn Vocabulary Word Search 4

Words are placed backwards, forward, diagonally, up and down. Words listed below are included in the maze. Circle the hidden vocabulary words in the maze.

```
R R D K D J X Z J Y L A N G U I S H T N
U Y N I I N Q N R W F A W A Y L A Y O V
M R R D S R C T H V B A P D E R R I C K
M P A Y P T L Z J R Z W G Y S M T B B S
A R K N O U R T E L L A P G P C S E P P
G P A S S E L A F F L I C T E D L R Y D
I M T D I O S K C O R F V R C D A T P R
N E E G T T M T X T L F R W U L H H N M
G L M M I R Q E T V E U A J L S B B S L
N O P L O L L E D Y S D J O A P D Y H D
I D E S N U D M J N D E C R T E I G R R
L E R O V A R S I I P L B L E T D O O L
B U A L V R N N N Y H D L Y Y R N N U W
R M N E B C N G F E U D A E A I A E D S
A H C M L E O F X U K A M N W F C S E N
W H E N K A U N Y K L D S C L I S N L G
L H V S C H M L F Q T A I O M E U R R N
M S I R E M S E M O C F D R R D B A U Z
H R J G J R H B N K U T M E K J L S F H
B H M Y H T L A E T S N B S L A I P N M
N C P R E J U D I C E D D G T K M Y U N
D O X O L O J E R L M D M H Y R E S R H
```

ABREAST	DISTRACTED	LOLLED	SHROUD
ADDLED	DOXOLOJER	MELODEUM	SOLEMN
AFFLICTED	ENCORES	MESMERISM	SPECULATE
BERTH	EVADE	MOURNFUL	STEALTHY
BRASH	FAGGED	PALLET	SUBLIME
BRISKEN	FEUD	PASSEL	SULTRY
BYGONES	FROCK	PETRIFIED	TEMPERANCE
CANDID	HAIL	PIOUS	UNFURLED
COLLAR	HUFFY	PREJUDICED	WADDING
CONFOUND	INSURRECTION	RANSACKED	WARBLING
DERRICK	LAMENTED	RANSOMED	WAYLAY
DISMAL	LANGUISH	RASPY	YAWL
DISPOSITION	LATH	RUMMAGING	

Huck Finn Vocabulary Word Search 4 Answer Key

Words are placed backwards, forward, diagonally, up and down. Words listed below are included in the maze. Circle the hidden vocabulary words in the maze.

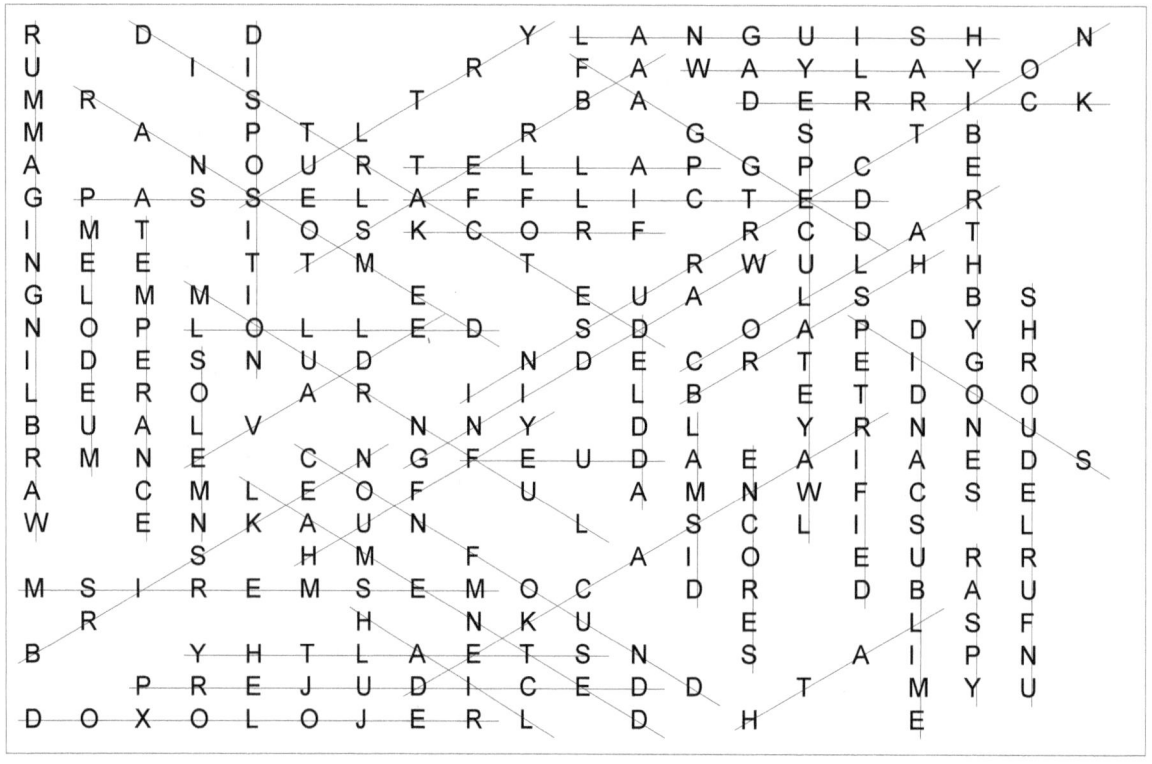

ABREAST	DISTRACTED	LOLLED	SHROUD
ADDLED	DOXOLOJER	MELODEUM	SOLEMN
AFFLICTED	ENCORES	MESMERISM	SPECULATE
BERTH	EVADE	MOURNFUL	STEALTHY
BRASH	FAGGED	PALLET	SUBLIME
BRISKEN	FEUD	PASSEL	SULTRY
BYGONES	FROCK	PETRIFIED	TEMPERANCE
CANDID	HAIL	PIOUS	UNFURLED
COLLAR	HUFFY	PREJUDICED	WADDING
CONFOUND	INSURRECTION	RANSACKED	WARBLING
DERRICK	LAMENTED	RANSOMED	WAYLAY
DISMAL	LANGUISH	RASPY	YAWL
DISPOSITION	LATH	RUMMAGING	

Huck Finn Vocabulary Crossword 1

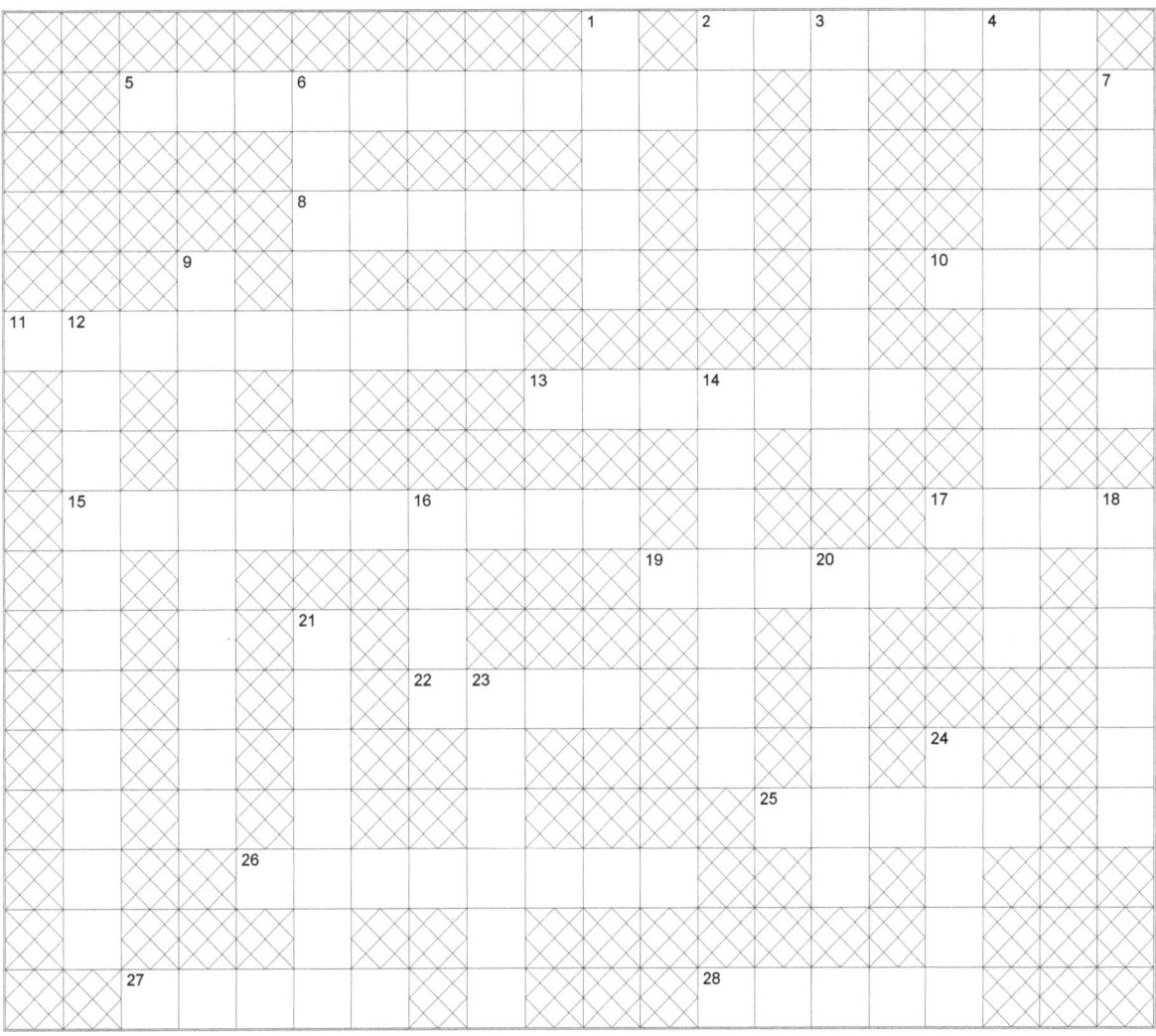

Across
2. Make more lively; brighten
5. Mercury
8. Relaxed
10. Small boat
11. Deserving admiration
13. Material for stopping charge in a gun
15. Reading a person's future by examining their skull
17. A hereditary fight
19. Woman's dress
22. Call to
25. Religious; reverent
26. Singing
27. Place to sleep
28. Grating; harsh

Down
1. Escape or avoid by cleverness or deceit
2. Uninhibited; tactless; impudent
3. Characterized by offensive boldness
4. Magic; sorcery
6. Seize or detain; grab and hold
7. Temporary bed made from bedding arranged on the floor
9. Pulled in conflicting emotional directions
12. Inclination; attitude
14. A crane
16. Building materials
18. Gloomy
20. Characterized by openness; straightforward
21. Side by side
23. Confused
24. Fit of anger or annoyance

Huck Finn Vocabulary Crossword 1 Answer Key

Across

2. Make more lively; brighten
5. Mercury
8. Relaxed
10. Small boat
11. Deserving admiration
13. Material for stopping charge in a gun
15. Reading a person's future by examining their skull
17. A hereditary fight
19. Woman's dress
22. Call to
25. Religious; reverent
26. Singing
27. Place to sleep
28. Grating; harsh

Down

1. Escape or avoid by cleverness or deceit
2. Uninhibited; tactless; impudent
3. Characterized by offensive boldness
4. Magic; sorcery
6. Seize or detain; grab and hold
7. Temporary bed made from bedding arranged on the floor
9. Pulled in conflicting emotional directions
12. Inclination; attitude
14. A crane
16. Building materials
18. Gloomy
20. Characterized by openness; straightforward
21. Side by side
23. Confused
24. Fit of anger or annoyance

Huck Finn Vocabulary Crossword 2

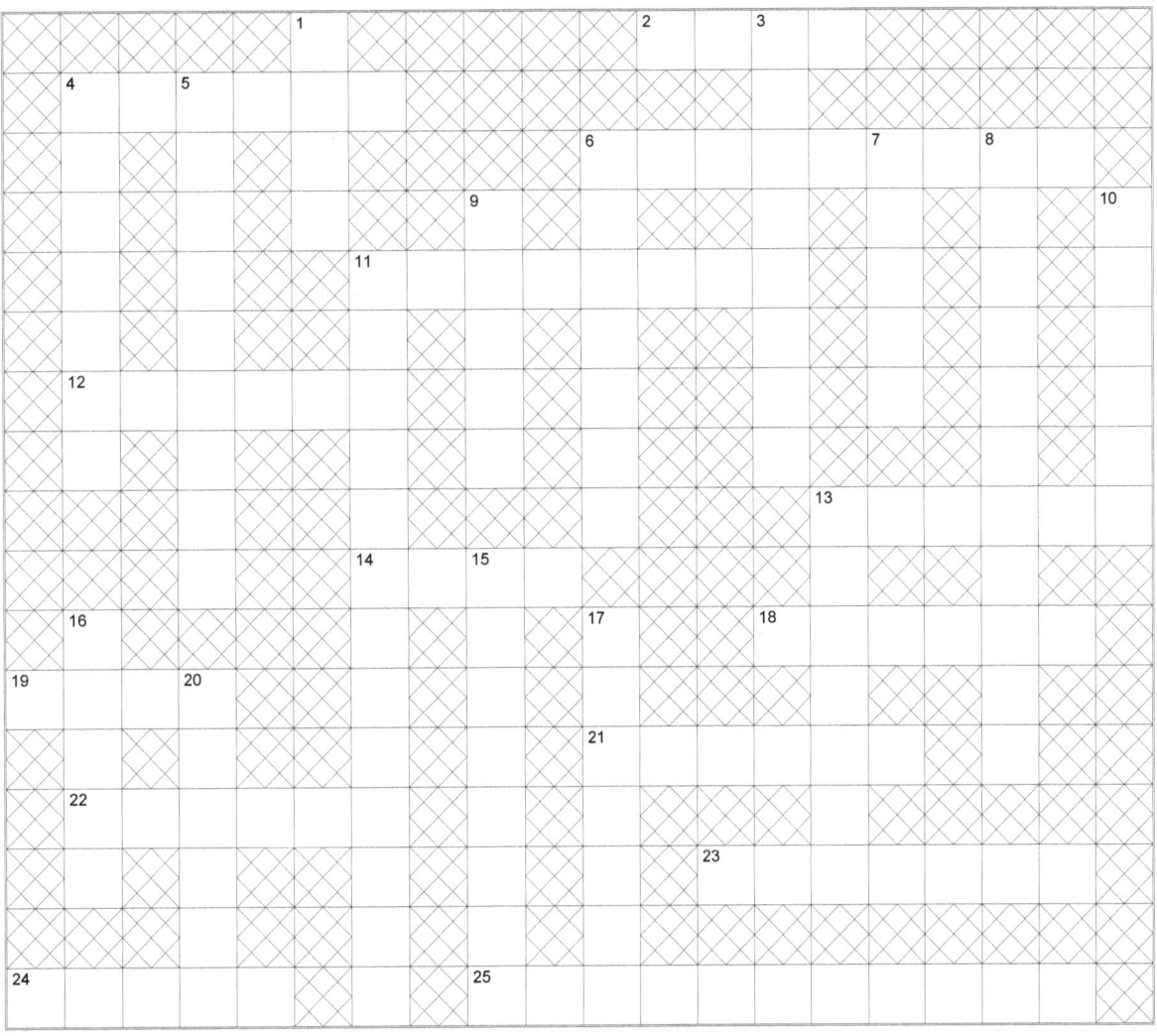

Across
2. Small boat
4. Gloomy
6. Turned to stone
11. Sad
12. Seize or detain; grab and hold
13. Very humid and hot
14. A hereditary fight
18. Exhausted
19. Call to
21. Characterized by openness; straightforward
22. Temporary bed made from bedding arranged on the floor
23. Past happenings
24. Escape or avoid by cleverness or deceit
25. Inclination; attitude

Down
1. Building materials
3. Singing
4. A crane
5. Make a risky financial transaction
6. Thoughtful
7. Woman's dress
8. Magic; sorcery
9. Fit of anger or annoyance
10. Lie in wait for and attack as in an ambush
11. Humiliation; embarrassment
13. Putting off; delaying
15. Spread out
16. Grating; harsh
17. Calls for repeat performances
20. Relaxed

Huck Finn Vocabulary Crossword 2 Answer Key

Across
2. Small boat
4. Gloomy
6. Turned to stone
11. Sad
12. Seize or detain; grab and hold
13. Very humid and hot
14. A hereditary fight
18. Exhausted
19. Call to
21. Characterized by openness; straightforward
22. Temporary bed made from bedding arranged on the floor
23. Past happenings
24. Escape or avoid by cleverness or deceit
25. Inclination; attitude

Down
1. Building materials
3. Singing
4. A crane
5. Make a risky financial transaction
6. Thoughtful
7. Woman's dress
8. Magic; sorcery
9. Fit of anger or annoyance
10. Lie in wait for and attack as in an ambush
11. Humiliation; embarrassment
13. Putting off; delaying
15. Spread out
16. Grating; harsh
17. Calls for repeat performances
20. Relaxed

Huck Finn Vocabulary Crossword 3

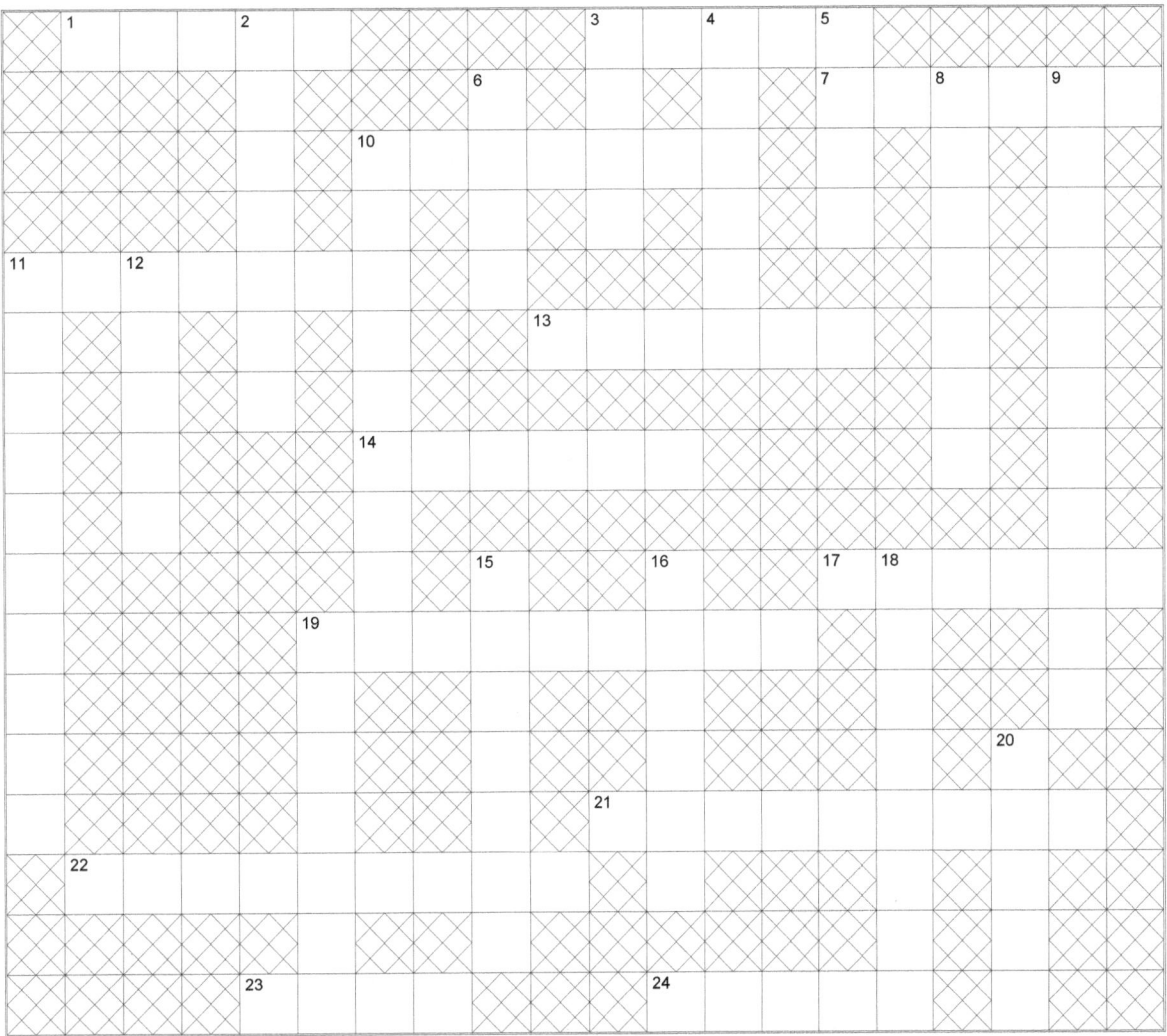

Across
1. Woman's dress
3. Fit of anger or annoyance
7. Confused
10. Putting off; delaying
11. Excellent; having a sense of grandeur
13. Characterized by openness; straightforward
14. Relaxed
17. Temporary bed made from bedding arranged on the floor
19. Turned to stone
21. Any of the powers possessed by the human mind
22. Handicapped
23. A hereditary fight
24. Escape or avoid by cleverness or deceit

Down
2. Obtaining by persistent persuasion
3. Call to
4. Exhausted
5. Small boat
6. Building materials
8. A crane
9. Magic; sorcery
10. Make a risky financial transaction
11. Holy
12. Uninhibited; tactless; impudent
15. Make more lively; brighten
16. Gloomy
18. Cut off
19. Thoughtful
20. Place to sleep

Huck Finn Vocabulary Crossword 3 Answer Key

Across
1. Woman's dress
3. Fit of anger or annoyance
7. Confused
10. Putting off; delaying
11. Excellent; having a sense of grandeur
13. Characterized by openness; straightforward
14. Relaxed
17. Temporary bed made from bedding arranged on the floor
19. Turned to stone
21. Any of the powers possessed by the human mind
22. Handicapped
23. A hereditary fight
24. Escape or avoid by cleverness or deceit

Down
2. Obtaining by persistent persuasion
3. Call to
4. Exhausted
5. Small boat
6. Building materials
8. A crane
9. Magic; sorcery
10. Make a risky financial transaction
11. Holy
12. Uninhibited; tactless; impudent
15. Make more lively; brighten
16. Gloomy
18. Cut off
19. Thoughtful
20. Place to sleep

Huck Finn Vocabulary Crossword 4

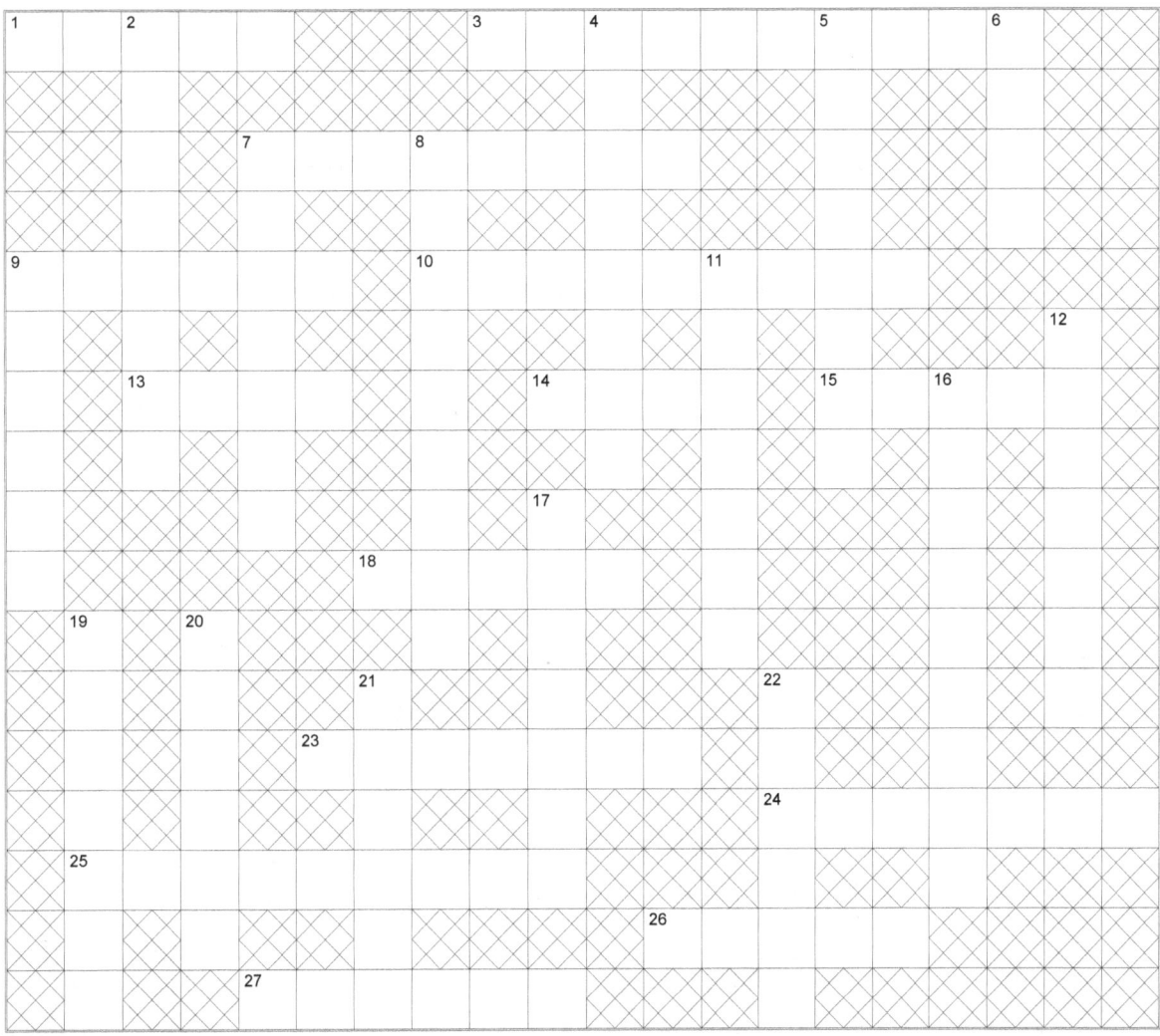

Across
1. Grating; harsh
3. Reading a person's future by examining their skull
7. Cause to become confused or perplexed
9. Seize or detain; grab and hold
10. Extravagant behavior
13. Call to
14. A hereditary fight
15. Escape or avoid by cleverness or deceit
18. Place to sleep
23. Material for stopping charge in a gun
24. Excellent; having a sense of grandeur
25. Rooting through as if searching
26. Uninhibited; tactless; impudent
27. Confused

Down
2. Acting with quiet caution
4. Freed from captivity for a price
5. Grieved
6. Small boat
7. Obtaining by persistent persuasion
8. Any of the powers possessed by the human mind
9. Characterized by openness; straightforward
11. Tiresome by reason of length; boring
12. Thoughtful
16. Deserving admiration
17. Putting off; delaying
19. Calls for repeat performances
20. Having a respectful calm
21. Exhausted
22. Gloomy

Huck Finn Vocabulary Crossword 4 Answer Key

Across
1. Grating; harsh
3. Reading a person's future by examining their skull
7. Cause to become confused or perplexed
9. Seize or detain; grab and hold
10. Extravagant behavior
13. Call to
14. A hereditary fight
15. Escape or avoid by cleverness or deceit
18. Place to sleep
23. Material for stopping charge in a gun
24. Excellent; having a sense of grandeur
25. Rooting through as if searching
26. Uninhibited; tactless; impudent
27. Confused

Down
2. Acting with quiet caution
4. Freed from captivity for a price
5. Grieved
6. Small boat
7. Obtaining by persistent persuasion
8. Any of the powers possessed by the human mind
9. Characterized by openness; straightforward
11. Tiresome by reason of length; boring
12. Thoughtful
16. Deserving admiration
17. Putting off; delaying
19. Calls for repeat performances
20. Having a respectful calm
21. Exhausted
22. Gloomy

Answers from grid:
1A. RASPY
3A. PHRENOLOGY
7A. CONFOUND
9A. COLLAR
10A. CAVORTING
13A. HAIL
14A. FEUD
15A. EVADE
18A. BERTH
23A. WADDING
24A. SUBLIME
25A. RUMMAGING
26A. BRASH
27A. ADDLED

2D. STEALTHY
4D. RANSOMED
5D. LAMENTED
6D. YAWL
7D. COAXING
8D. FACULTIES
9D. CANDID
11D. TEDIOUS
12D. PENSIVE
16D. ADMIRABLE
17D. STALLING
19D. ENCORES
20D. SOLEMN
21D. FAGGED
22D. DISMAL

102

Huck Finn Vocabulary Juggle Letters 1

1. SILAMD = 1. _____
   Gloomy

2. NOLMSE = 2. _____
   Having a respectful calm

3. DCEIIATFNS = 3. _____
   Holy

4. EURUNDFL = 4. _____
   Spread out

5. IDPMNETU = 5. _____
   Characterized by offensive boldness

6. KEBRINS = 6. _____
   Make more lively; brighten

7. DEFU = 7. _____
   A hereditary fight

8. LEADMAIRB = 8. _____
   Deserving admiration

9. STDOINIIPOS = 9. _____
   Inclination; attitude

10. IEDCDPEJUR =10. _____
    Having a preconceived preference

11. HSNIUALG =11. _____
    Faint; feeble; sickly

12. HRSBA =12. _____
    Uninhibited; tactless; impudent

13. OENMDECMC =13. _____
    Began

14. OALLCR =14. _____
    Seize or detain; grab and hold

15. AHTL =15. _____
    Building materials

Huck Finn Vocabulary Juggle Letters 1 Answer Key

1. SILAMD = 1. DISMAL
Gloomy

2. NOLMSE = 2. SOLEMN
Having a respectful calm

3. DCEIIATFNS = 3. SANCTIFIED
Holy

4. EURUNDFL = 4. UNFURLED
Spread out

5. IDPMNETU = 5. IMPUDENT
Characterized by offensive boldness

6. KEBRINS = 6. BRISKEN
Make more lively; brighten

7. DEFU = 7. FEUD
A hereditary fight

8. LEADMAIRB = 8. ADMIRABLE
Deserving admiration

9. STDOINIIPOS = 9. DISPOSITION
Inclination; attitude

10. IEDCDPEJUR = 10. PREJUDICED
Having a preconceived preference

11. HSNIUALG = 11. LANGUISH
Faint; feeble; sickly

12. HRSBA = 12. BRASH
Uninhibited; tactless; impudent

13. OENMDECMC = 13. COMMENCED
Began

14. OALLCR = 14. COLLAR
Seize or detain; grab and hold

15. AHTL = 15. LATH
Building materials

Huck Finn Vocabulary Juggle Letters 2

1. SAESPL = 1. _____
   Bunch

2. IRBENSK = 2. _____
   Make more lively; brighten

3. CFKOR = 3. _____
   Woman's dress

4. ISOUP = 4. _____
   Religious; reverent

5. MLOENS = 5. _____
   Having a respectful calm

6. OSDTUEI = 6. _____
   Tiresome by reason of length; boring

7. TEANLEDM = 7. _____
   Grieved

8. NTCRPAEEEM = 8. _____
   Moderation; sobriety

9. LOXOJDROE = 9. _____
   Kind of hymn

10. BMLISEU =10. _____
    Excellent; having a sense of grandeur

11. GBRAWILN =11. _____
    Singing

12. NXAIOCG =12. _____
    Obtaining by persistent persuasion

13. DEINMTPU =13. _____
    Characterized by offensive boldness

14. FYUHF =14. _____
    Fit of anger or annoyance

15. DDDLEA =15. _____
    Confused

Huck Finn Vocabulary Juggle Letters 2 Answer Key

1. SAESPL = 1. PASSEL
Bunch

2. IRBENSK = 2. BRISKEN
Make more lively; brighten

3. CFKOR = 3. FROCK
Woman's dress

4. ISOUP = 4. PIOUS
Religious; reverent

5. MLOENS = 5. SOLEMN
Having a respectful calm

6. OSDTUEI = 6. TEDIOUS
Tiresome by reason of length; boring

7. TEANLEDM = 7. LAMENTED
Grieved

8. NTCRPAEEEM = 8. TEMPERANCE
Moderation; sobriety

9. LOXOJDROE = 9. DOXOLOJER
Kind of hymn

10. BMLISEU = 10. SUBLIME
Excellent; having a sense of grandeur

11. GBRAWILN = 11. WARBLING
Singing

12. NXAIOCG = 12. COAXING
Obtaining by persistent persuasion

13. DEINMTPU = 13. IMPUDENT
Characterized by offensive boldness

14. FYUHF = 14. HUFFY
Fit of anger or annoyance

15. DDDLEA = 15. ADDLED
Confused

Huck Finn Vocabulary Juggle Letters 3

1. USPIO = 1. _____
   Religious; reverent

2. KDERCRI = 2. _____
   A crane

3. REEIDPJUDC = 3. _____
   Having a preconceived preference

4. EVSNIEP = 4. _____
   Thoughtful

5. RNSKIEB = 5. _____
   Make more lively; brighten

6. FATTOIRCIIMON = 6. _____
   Humiliation; embarrassment

7. YHFUF = 7. _____
   Fit of anger or annoyance

8. PERANMTEEC = 8. _____
   Moderation; sobriety

9. DNDACI = 9. _____
   Characterized by openness; straightforward

10. UMELEDOM =10. _____
    Small reed organ

11. UCAELSPET =11. _____
    Make a risky financial transaction

12. RUNLEDFU =12. _____
    Spread out

13. CLSAUTIV =13. _____
    Food

14. AEGGFD =14. _____
    Exhausted

15. LIBNGARW =15. _____
    Singing

Huck Finn Vocabulary Juggle Letters 3 Answer Key

1. USPIO = 1. PIOUS
Religious; reverent

2. KDERCRI = 2. DERRICK
A crane

3. REEIDPJUDC = 3. PREJUDICED
Having a preconceived preference

4. EVSNIEP = 4. PENSIVE
Thoughtful

5. RNSKIEB = 5. BRISKEN
Make more lively; brighten

6. FATTOIRCIIMON = 6. MORTIFICATION
Humiliation; embarrassment

7. YHFUF = 7. HUFFY
Fit of anger or annoyance

8. PERANMTEEC = 8. TEMPERANCE
Moderation; sobriety

9. DNDACI = 9. CANDID
Characterized by openness; straightforward

10. UMELEDOM = 10. MELODEUM
Small reed organ

11. UCAELSPET = 11. SPECULATE
Make a risky financial transaction

12. RUNLEDFU = 12. UNFURLED
Spread out

13. CLSAUTIV = 13. VICTUALS
Food

14. AEGGFD = 14. FAGGED
Exhausted

15. LIBNGARW = 15. WARBLING
Singing

Huck Finn Vocabulary Juggle Letters 4

1. LBWGANRI = 1. _____
   Singing

2. OHRUDS = 2. _____
   Cloth used to wrap a body for burial

3. NOSTNIHAC = 3. _____
   Post of timber or iron for support

4. IPUSO = 4. _____
   Religious; reverent

5. OSISNITIDTCN = 5. _____
   Differences

6. UTNMIPDE = 6. _____
   Characterized by offensive boldness

7. DMENALET = 7. _____
   Grieved

8. ESIUMLB = 8. _____
   Excellent; having a sense of grandeur

9. CORLAL = 9. _____
   Seize or detain; grab and hold

10. BOSIQEUSE =10. _____
    Funeral rites

11. LETLAP =11. _____
    Temporary bed made from bedding arranged on the floor

12. IFTIANCDSE =12. _____
    Holy

13. ESMOLN =13. _____
    Having a respectful calm

14. RLUMFOUN =14. _____
    Sad

15. DCANDI =15. _____
    Characterized by openness; straightforward

Huck Finn Vocabulary Juggle Letters 4 Answer Key

1. LBWGANRI = 1. WARBLING
Singing

2. OHRUDS = 2. SHROUD
Cloth used to wrap a body for burial

3. NOSTNIHAC = 3. STANCHION
Post of timber or iron for support

4. IPUSO = 4. PIOUS
Religious; reverent

5. OSISNITIDTCN = 5. DISTINCTIONS
Differences

6. UTNMIPDE = 6. IMPUDENT
Characterized by offensive boldness

7. DMENALET = 7. LAMENTED
Grieved

8. ESIUMLB = 8. SUBLIME
Excellent; having a sense of grandeur

9. CORLAL = 9. COLLAR
Seize or detain; grab and hold

10. BOSIQEUSE = 10. OBSEQUIES
Funeral rites

11. LETLAP = 11. PALLET
Temporary bed made from bedding arranged on the floor

12. IFTIANCDSE = 12. SANCTIFIED
Holy

13. ESMOLN = 13. SOLEMN
Having a respectful calm

14. RLUMFOUN = 14. MOURNFUL
Sad

15. DCANDI = 15. CANDID
Characterized by openness; straightforward

ABOLITIONIST	Person against slavery
ABREAST	Side by side
ADDLED	Confused
ADMIRABLE	Deserving admiration
AFFLICTED	Handicapped
AMPUTATE	Cut off
BERTH	Place to sleep

BRASH	Uninhibited; tactless; impudent
BRISKEN	Make more lively; brighten
BYGONES	Past happenings
CANDID	Characterized by openness; straightforward
CAVORTING	Extravagant behavior
COAXING	Obtaining by persistent persuasion
COLLAR	Seize or detain; grab and hold

COMMENCED	Began
CONFOUND	Cause to become confused or perplexed
CONVENIENCES	Things that increase comfort or save work
COUNTERFEIT	Fake; not real
DERRICK	A crane
DISMAL	Gloomy
DISPOSITION	Inclination; attitude

DISTINCTIONS	Differences
DISTRACTED	Pulled in conflicting emotional directions
DOXOLOJER	Kind of hymn
ENCHANTMENT	Magic; sorcery
ENCORES	Calls for repeat performances
EVADE	Escape or avoid by cleverness or deceit
FACULTIES	Any of the powers possessed by the human mind

FAGGED	Exhausted
FEUD	A hereditary fight
FROCK	Woman's dress
HAIL	Call to
HUFFY	Fit of anger or annoyance
IMPUDENT	Characterized by offensive boldness
INSURRECTION	Act or instance of open revolt

LAMENTED	Grieved
LANGUISH	Faint; feeble; sickly
LATH	Building materials
LOLLED	Relaxed
MELODEUM	Small reed organ
MESMERISM	Hypnotism
MORTIFICATION	Humiliation; embarrassment

MOURNFUL	Sad
OBSEQUIES	Funeral rites
PALAVERING	Making idle talk
PALLET	Temporary bed made from bedding arranged on the floor
PASSEL	Bunch
PENSIVE	Thoughtful
PETRIFIED	Turned to stone

PHRENOLOGY	Reading a person's future by examining their skull
PIOUS	Religious; reverent
PREJUDICED	Having a preconceived preference
QUICKSILVER	Mercury
RANSACKED	Searched thoroughly but hastily
RANSOMED	Freed from captivity for a price
RASPY	Grating; harsh

RUMMAGING	Rooting through as if searching
SANCTIFIED	Holy
SHROUD	Cloth used to wrap a body for burial
SOLEMN	Having a respectful calm
SOLILOQUY	Dramatic monologue
SPECULATE	Make a risky financial transaction
STANCHION	Post of timber or iron for support

STAVING	Putting off; delaying
STEALTHY	Acting with quiet caution
SUBLIME	Excellent; having a sense of grandeur
SULTRY	Very humid and hot
TEDIOUS	Tiresome by reason of length; boring
TEMPERANCE	Moderation; sobriety
UNFURLED	Spread out

VICTUALS	Food
WADDING	Material for stopping charge in a gun
WARBLING	Singing
WAYLAY	Lie in wait for and attack as in an ambush
YAWL	Small boat

Huck Finn Vocabulary

HAIL	COLLAR	MELODEUM	ENCORES	FEUD
SANCTIFIED	LOLLED	SOLILOQUY	VICTUALS	ABOLITIONIST
PHRENOLOGY	TEMPERANCE	FREE SPACE	WADDING	FROCK
RUMMAGING	COMMENCED	DERRICK	STANCHION	UNFURLED
ENCHANTMENT	COAXING	CANDID	LATH	BRISKEN

Huck Finn Vocabulary

PIOUS	PALAVERING	SHROUD	DISMAL	QUICKSILVER
PREJUDICED	EVADE	PETRIFIED	IMPUDENT	MORTIFICATION
PENSIVE	RASPY	FREE SPACE	BERTH	BYGONES
SOLEMN	STAVING	DISTINCTIONS	DOXOLOJER	SULTRY
RANSACKED	FAGGED	SPECULATE	DISPOSITION	AFFLICTED

Huck Finn Vocabulary

PHRENOLOGY	HAIL	SHROUD	BERTH	RANSOMED
OBSEQUIES	FEUD	AFFLICTED	CONVENIENCES	CAVORTING
DERRICK	BYGONES	FREE SPACE	DISMAL	MORTIFICATION
SUBLIME	COMMENCED	SOLEMN	IMPUDENT	ENCORES
YAWL	INSURRECTION	DISPOSITION	CONFOUND	LAMENTED

Huck Finn Vocabulary

WARBLING	COLLAR	FAGGED	TEDIOUS	MESMERISM
QUICKSILVER	RANSACKED	SULTRY	COUNTERFEIT	PIOUS
WADDING	SOLILOQUY	FREE SPACE	DISTRACTED	CANDID
EVADE	MOURNFUL	MELODEUM	BRASH	STEALTHY
LATH	SPECULATE	PALLET	FROCK	AMPUTATE

Huck Finn Vocabulary

ADDLED	SULTRY	FEUD	PENSIVE	SHROUD
STEALTHY	LATH	SOLEMN	DISTINCTIONS	VICTUALS
HUFFY	ADMIRABLE	FREE SPACE	FAGGED	AFFLICTED
PALLET	ABOLITIONIST	SPECULATE	MORTIFICATION	ENCHANTMENT
DISPOSITION	LOLLED	RUMMAGING	CONVENIENCES	SOLILOQUY

Huck Finn Vocabulary

SANCTIFIED	SUBLIME	LANGUISH	DERRICK	MELODEUM
FACULTIES	ABREAST	RANSOMED	UNFURLED	PIOUS
PALAVERING	AMPUTATE	FREE SPACE	RANSACKED	PHRENOLOGY
STANCHION	IMPUDENT	COLLAR	CONFOUND	ENCORES
DOXOLOJER	MOURNFUL	MESMERISM	TEMPERANCE	WADDING

Huck Finn Vocabulary

CONVENIENCES	VICTUALS	BYGONES	DISPOSITION	LOLLED
DISMAL	ENCHANTMENT	RASPY	RANSACKED	TEMPERANCE
SOLILOQUY	COUNTERFEIT	FREE SPACE	FROCK	BERTH
SHROUD	FACULTIES	SUBLIME	YAWL	WARBLING
PETRIFIED	LATH	PREJUDICED	LAMENTED	HUFFY

Huck Finn Vocabulary

RANSOMED	RUMMAGING	MESMERISM	MORTIFICATION	ABREAST
ADMIRABLE	TEDIOUS	CONFOUND	SULTRY	HAIL
SANCTIFIED	STEALTHY	FREE SPACE	PALAVERING	CAVORTING
ENCORES	STAVING	DOXOLOJER	SOLEMN	BRASH
AMPUTATE	WAYLAY	PALLET	PHRENOLOGY	LANGUISH

Huck Finn Vocabulary

SOLILOQUY	TEDIOUS	PALLET	PENSIVE	WARBLING
ENCHANTMENT	STANCHION	PETRIFIED	HUFFY	DERRICK
MELODEUM	COLLAR	FREE SPACE	COMMENCED	SUBLIME
STEALTHY	RASPY	RUMMAGING	LOLLED	IMPUDENT
COUNTERFEIT	TEMPERANCE	LAMENTED	BERTH	FACULTIES

Huck Finn Vocabulary

MORTIFICATION	ABOLITIONIST	SOLEMN	BRASH	SHROUD
FEUD	WAYLAY	COAXING	INSURRECTION	SULTRY
ADDLED	EVADE	FREE SPACE	ADMIRABLE	PHRENOLOGY
DISPOSITION	BRISKEN	CONVENIENCES	WADDING	RANSACKED
PIOUS	FAGGED	DOXOLOJER	HAIL	LATH

Huck Finn Vocabulary

LOLLED	DOXOLOJER	AMPUTATE	IMPUDENT	BERTH
COMMENCED	ABREAST	CONVENIENCES	RUMMAGING	PALLET
UNFURLED	SOLEMN	FREE SPACE	ENCORES	QUICKSILVER
FROCK	SANCTIFIED	LAMENTED	PIOUS	CAVORTING
MORTIFICATION	SULTRY	DERRICK	CANDID	PETRIFIED

Huck Finn Vocabulary

RANSACKED	DISMAL	FAGGED	BYGONES	OBSEQUIES
COLLAR	FACULTIES	SUBLIME	LANGUISH	PREJUDICED
DISTINCTIONS	ENCHANTMENT	FREE SPACE	TEMPERANCE	RASPY
STEALTHY	ABOLITIONIST	PALAVERING	FEUD	LATH
VICTUALS	PENSIVE	ADMIRABLE	HAIL	WAYLAY

Huck Finn Vocabulary

ADDLED	DISTRACTED	LATH	SANCTIFIED	PIOUS
LAMENTED	DOXOLOJER	COAXING	IMPUDENT	RASPY
EVADE	SUBLIME	FREE SPACE	RANSACKED	FEUD
SHROUD	FAGGED	PHRENOLOGY	HAIL	MOURNFUL
BRASH	PETRIFIED	COLLAR	STANCHION	STAVING

Huck Finn Vocabulary

WARBLING	VICTUALS	ADMIRABLE	LOLLED	COMMENCED
PALLET	HUFFY	CANDID	RANSOMED	DERRICK
COUNTERFEIT	WADDING	FREE SPACE	TEMPERANCE	CONFOUND
MESMERISM	DISPOSITION	TEDIOUS	MELODEUM	STEALTHY
DISTINCTIONS	SOLILOQUY	SPECULATE	BRISKEN	FACULTIES

Huck Finn Vocabulary

CAVORTING	LOLLED	ABOLITIONIST	DISPOSITION	OBSEQUIES
RANSOMED	HAIL	MOURNFUL	QUICKSILVER	PREJUDICED
RUMMAGING	HUFFY	FREE SPACE	PHRENOLOGY	CONVENIENCES
MELODEUM	LATH	UNFURLED	PIOUS	PETRIFIED
ADDLED	YAWL	FACULTIES	COUNTERFEIT	BRISKEN

Huck Finn Vocabulary

FROCK	COMMENCED	PALLET	CANDID	BRASH
BERTH	COAXING	SOLILOQUY	DERRICK	COLLAR
LANGUISH	WAYLAY	FREE SPACE	SULTRY	ABREAST
STANCHION	TEDIOUS	ENCORES	STEALTHY	AMPUTATE
WADDING	WARBLING	SOLEMN	SHROUD	DISTRACTED

Huck Finn Vocabulary

HAIL	TEDIOUS	RANSOMED	DISPOSITION	YAWL
WADDING	FROCK	OBSEQUIES	MORTIFICATION	SPECULATE
LAMENTED	QUICKSILVER	FREE SPACE	IMPUDENT	CAVORTING
ABREAST	COLLAR	PIOUS	ADDLED	RASPY
SHROUD	FACULTIES	RUMMAGING	ABOLITIONIST	DISTRACTED

Huck Finn Vocabulary

STEALTHY	DOXOLOJER	LOLLED	INSURRECTION	EVADE
CONFOUND	BYGONES	STANCHION	DERRICK	CONVENIENCES
SOLILOQUY	COUNTERFEIT	FREE SPACE	AMPUTATE	FEUD
TEMPERANCE	ADMIRABLE	MOURNFUL	SUBLIME	WARBLING
PALAVERING	SANCTIFIED	ENCORES	CANDID	SOLEMN

Huck Finn Vocabulary

SOLEMN	SANCTIFIED	MORTIFICATION	WAYLAY	MESMERISM
LANGUISH	CANDID	MELODEUM	BERTH	STANCHION
CONFOUND	INSURRECTION	FREE SPACE	SUBLIME	PREJUDICED
ENCHANTMENT	ABOLITIONIST	PALLET	RANSACKED	FAGGED
COAXING	PASSEL	SPECULATE	FEUD	RANSOMED

Huck Finn Vocabulary

STEALTHY	COLLAR	PENSIVE	HAIL	ADMIRABLE
CAVORTING	PALAVERING	BYGONES	OBSEQUIES	DISTRACTED
PIOUS	WARBLING	FREE SPACE	AMPUTATE	DOXOLOJER
TEMPERANCE	EVADE	CONVENIENCES	IMPUDENT	UNFURLED
SULTRY	COMMENCED	PHRENOLOGY	YAWL	RUMMAGING

Huck Finn Vocabulary

SULTRY	CANDID	ADMIRABLE	RASPY	DERRICK
TEDIOUS	PIOUS	COAXING	RANSACKED	CONVENIENCES
COLLAR	LATH	FREE SPACE	RANSOMED	MELODEUM
BRASH	PASSEL	HUFFY	SUBLIME	UNFURLED
STANCHION	ENCORES	BERTH	TEMPERANCE	INSURRECTION

Huck Finn Vocabulary

PREJUDICED	COMMENCED	ADDLED	WAYLAY	IMPUDENT
FAGGED	COUNTERFEIT	HAIL	BRISKEN	CAVORTING
SHROUD	PALLET	FREE SPACE	PHRENOLOGY	LOLLED
OBSEQUIES	DISTINCTIONS	WADDING	VICTUALS	YAWL
ENCHANTMENT	FACULTIES	SOLILOQUY	RUMMAGING	STEALTHY

Huck Finn Vocabulary

CANDID	COUNTERFEIT	PALLET	DISMAL	BERTH
ENCORES	CONVENIENCES	SUBLIME	SOLEMN	AMPUTATE
PHRENOLOGY	RASPY	FREE SPACE	ADDLED	WADDING
ADMIRABLE	COAXING	DERRICK	RUMMAGING	HAIL
CONFOUND	FROCK	MOURNFUL	FAGGED	FACULTIES

Huck Finn Vocabulary

LANGUISH	ABREAST	DOXOLOJER	SULTRY	VICTUALS
MORTIFICATION	WAYLAY	RANSOMED	INSURRECTION	STEALTHY
YAWL	BRASH	FREE SPACE	HUFFY	AFFLICTED
CAVORTING	PREJUDICED	MESMERISM	PENSIVE	SOLILOQUY
DISTINCTIONS	PETRIFIED	BYGONES	STAVING	DISPOSITION

Huck Finn Vocabulary

COMMENCED	MELODEUM	PETRIFIED	COLLAR	SULTRY
STEALTHY	CONVENIENCES	RASPY	FAGGED	ADDLED
HUFFY	FEUD	FREE SPACE	PENSIVE	CAVORTING
DISPOSITION	LATH	ENCORES	AMPUTATE	WARBLING
SOLILOQUY	TEDIOUS	PALLET	YAWL	LAMENTED

Huck Finn Vocabulary

WADDING	INSURRECTION	COAXING	STAVING	BERTH
HAIL	SHROUD	DISMAL	WAYLAY	AFFLICTED
ABOLITIONIST	EVADE	FREE SPACE	MOURNFUL	FROCK
SANCTIFIED	LOLLED	LANGUISH	DERRICK	RANSOMED
CONFOUND	BRISKEN	QUICKSILVER	OBSEQUIES	SOLEMN

Huck Finn Vocabulary

UNFURLED	CAVORTING	SANCTIFIED	STANCHION	CONFOUND
COMMENCED	RUMMAGING	AMPUTATE	RASPY	PALAVERING
PIOUS	PENSIVE	FREE SPACE	SOLEMN	TEMPERANCE
BYGONES	COLLAR	ABREAST	YAWL	DISTINCTIONS
IMPUDENT	MOURNFUL	STAVING	AFFLICTED	LATH

Huck Finn Vocabulary

ABOLITIONIST	MESMERISM	HAIL	PETRIFIED	EVADE
LANGUISH	ENCORES	SUBLIME	DISPOSITION	COAXING
BERTH	MORTIFICATION	FREE SPACE	FACULTIES	CONVENIENCES
INSURRECTION	RANSACKED	FAGGED	ADDLED	HUFFY
SHROUD	STEALTHY	FROCK	WADDING	DISTRACTED

Huck Finn Vocabulary

ENCHANTMENT	LANGUISH	COAXING	SANCTIFIED	FEUD
WADDING	ADMIRABLE	SULTRY	ABREAST	WAYLAY
STANCHION	MOURNFUL	FREE SPACE	ADDLED	FAGGED
RANSACKED	PHRENOLOGY	COLLAR	INSURRECTION	TEDIOUS
DISPOSITION	PIOUS	RASPY	LATH	HAIL

Huck Finn Vocabulary

FROCK	COMMENCED	CAVORTING	SOLEMN	UNFURLED
CANDID	LAMENTED	DISMAL	COUNTERFEIT	FACULTIES
PREJUDICED	STEALTHY	FREE SPACE	PASSEL	PETRIFIED
DISTINCTIONS	SOLILOQUY	EVADE	PALAVERING	WARBLING
BRASH	AFFLICTED	PENSIVE	AMPUTATE	PALLET

Huck Finn Vocabulary

YAWL	SULTRY	LATH	WARBLING	STANCHION
PENSIVE	BYGONES	DOXOLOJER	DISPOSITION	DERRICK
COLLAR	LANGUISH	FREE SPACE	CANDID	TEDIOUS
STEALTHY	MELODEUM	OBSEQUIES	EVADE	PHRENOLOGY
DISTRACTED	ADDLED	UNFURLED	VICTUALS	LOLLED

Huck Finn Vocabulary

PIOUS	AFFLICTED	CAVORTING	DISTINCTIONS	COUNTERFEIT
AMPUTATE	ABREAST	MOURNFUL	PALLET	QUICKSILVER
FROCK	HAIL	FREE SPACE	SOLEMN	ENCORES
INSURRECTION	RANSOMED	PASSEL	RANSACKED	FEUD
BERTH	ADMIRABLE	PREJUDICED	DISMAL	CONFOUND

www.ingramcontent.com/pod-product-compliance
Lightning Source LLC
LaVergne TN
LVHW081537060526
838200LV00048B/2119

9781602493438